SEIZING GOD'S PROMISES FEARLESSLY

A Study of Joshua

ILEANA SEWARD

WESTBOW
PRESS®
A DIVISION OF THOMAS NELSON
& ZONDERVAN

Scriptures taken from the Holy Bible, New International Version®, NIV®. Copyright © 1973, 1978, 1984, 2011 by Biblica, Inc.™ Used by permission of Zondervan. All rights reserved worldwide. www.zondervan.com The "NIV" and "New International Version" are trademarks registered in the United States Patent and Trademark Office by Biblica, Inc.™

WestBow Press books may be ordered through booksellers or by contacting:

WestBow Press
A Division of Thomas Nelson & Zondervan
1663 Liberty Drive
Bloomington, IN 47403
www.westbowpress.com
1 (866) 928-1240

Because of the dynamic nature of the Internet, any web addresses or links contained in this book may have changed since publication and may no longer be valid. The views expressed in this work are solely those of the author and do not necessarily reflect the views of the publisher, and the publisher hereby disclaims any responsibility for them.

Any people depicted in stock imagery provided by Getty Images are models, and such images are being used for illustrative purposes only. Certain stock imagery © Getty Images.

ISBN: 978-1-9736-5970-9 (sc)
ISBN: 978-1-9736-5971-6 (e)

Print information available on the last page.

WestBow Press rev. date: 04/15/2019

I dedicate this Bible study to those who encouraged me to make it happen!

My husband, son, and daughter encouraged me, supported me, humored me, wrestled through Scripture with me, and are just plain amazing people. Ron, Jimmy, Katie – I love you!

My mom, Tess Torres, thinks I'm brilliant, and told me I *have* to finish this project. She got me my first study Bible not knowing I would wear out it's binding. I love you, mom!

My mother-in-law, Mary Ann Seward, gave me my first grownup Bible (no pictures!) years before I had any idea how precious that book would become in my life.

Several women in my Sunday School class at Countryside Church of the Nazarene, in Lebanon, Ohio went through this study week by week as I was writing it. Their encouragement and feedback kept me pounding away at the keyboard turning research and notes into a Bible study.

Amanda Penman, Ashley Fornshell, Debbie Bell, Debbie Jayne, Donna Morhous, Jenni Arns, Jenny Embleton, Linda Besecker, Marsha Jones, Monica Hale, and Vickie Cundiff – thank you for encouraging me!

Thanks to Rev. Carrie McIntosh, master of the English language, for agreeing to be my editor. I am grateful for your feedback and encouragement and attention to detail!

Rev. Sheila Slone, a pastor I greatly admire, took me to lunch one day. As I lamented a lack of opportunity to build my preaching muscles, she gave me advice including these words: "… and until then, maybe you need to just write it down. Share the word God gave you that way."

My accountability partner, Rev. Angela France, gave me daily encouragement and let me bounce ideas off her. She was the bold friend who listened to me pour out my heart one day, and simply said, "Pen to paper, sister." Angela, thank you for being a true encourager!

Contents

Welcome!

Welcome to *the Seizing God's Promises Fearlessly* Bible study! We're about to spend six weeks studying the conquest of the Promised Land, and many lessons from Joshua and the people he led.

For six weeks, there are five daily homework assignments followed by a group discussion note space. This page indicates questions from the homework intended to spark meaningful group discussion. There is a Group Study Leader's Guide at the back of this book to help your group's facilitator(s).

As you go through each day's homework, mark questions that you feel would be valuable to discuss or share when you gather with your study group. Underline or highlight any text you feel would be worth discussing or sharing with anyone who may have missed a day's assignment.

You may notice I did not quote much Scripture in these pages, and that was no accident, my friend. I want you do open the pages of your Bible and find them. The discoveries are so much better when you make them yourself! Any time I do reference Scripture, it comes from the NIV, mostly because that was the beloved, worn, pocket sized Bible that went everywhere with me for months and months as I studied and wrote. Use whichever translation you prefer.

The pages of Joshua have become a place for me to camp and learn, and to allow God to heal and encourage me. A book about war was the last place I expected to find healing and peace, but isn't that how God likes to work?

Throughout Joshua, God drives home the command: Do not fear! Be strong! Be courageous! He follows that with a promise as the empowerment to obey His command: Because the Lord your God is with you. Joshua's testimony – after he was delivered from slavery, his faithfulness was discounted by his community, he wandered the desert for forty years, he crossed Jordan into the Promised Land, and fought for the better part of forty-five more years – is that God is good!

Not one of God's good promises has failed!

I want to approach my last days on earth with the same confident proclamation: God is good, and all of His promises are true!

Fear has been a frequent companion of mine throughout my life. So have self-doubt, insecurity, and a feeling that I have no idea what to do next. God has used Joshua to teach me. He has used Joshua to call me to the mat on a few things, but Almighty Comforter that He is, He picked me up off the mat, drew me close, and pointed to victory in Him. Praise God!

Intro to Bible Study
The Story of God from
Genesis to Joshua

Today is dedicated to the brand new student of the Bible!

If you are one of the people who say, "I've never read the Bible," or, "I've never done a Bible study," or, "I have no idea what I'm getting myself into," then today is for you! And it will be an easy day! If you're not in that boat, read it anyway, so you are reminded of where some people are starting.

I became a Christian as an adult, and I will never forget how dumb I felt in my first Bible study when the leader said to open up to whatever verse it was. I didn't know where on earth to search in that giant book! I didn't realize it then, but that didn't make me dumb – it's like anything else in life: the longer you use something, the more familiar it becomes!

Lesson 1: Use your table of contents! If you want to make it less obvious, use a tiny flag sticker or post-it to mark the Table of Contents page so you can find what you need. I promise, no one else is looking to see if you find a certain verse faster than they do.

Another helpful hint: the book of Psalms is pretty much in the middle of the Bible, highlight that on your contents page, and you'll be able to look before or after it quickly.

Right now, grab your Bible, and find your Table of Contents.

Look for the following books: Exodus, Numbers, Joshua.

Lesson 2: The larger numbers in each book are the Chapter numbers, and the smaller ones are verses. For example, when you see Joshua 1:9, you should go to the book of Joshua, look for Chapter 1, and scroll down to verse 9.

If anything else seems foreign to you, please don't hesitate to ask your study leader – it is the leader's job and pleasure to help you learn!

To prepare you for this study, I'm going to give you a rushed version of the history so you have a sense of what is going on when we begin to study Joshua. Today and tomorrow, we will take a close look at the family drama among the 12 men whose offspring would later make up the tribes of Israel.

Early in the story of God and humanity, God chose a man named Abraham with whom He made a covenant (a binding promise). He promised to be Abraham's God, and to multiply Abraham's offspring into many nations, and to bless the whole world through his lineage (through Jesus) if Abraham would be faithful to Him. He also promised Abraham specific land (later known as Israel) as the inheritance to Abraham's offspring. Abraham entered into that covenant, as did his son Isaac, and Isaac's son Jacob, and Jacob's 12 sons, and the generations to follow.

Isaac and his wife, Rebekah had twin sons named Jacob and Esau. Jacob was the son whose line would inherit God's covenant. There was more than a little bit of sibling rivalry between the twins, and when Jacob had angered his brother enough that he feared for his life, Jacob fled to live with his uncle, Laban.

This moment in time is where we pick up our study of the 12 sons who became the patriarchs of the tribes of Israel, but first, we need to peek ahead at an important name change.

Read Genesis 32:27-28. Whose name changed? What is his new name?

Read Genesis 29:14-30:24, and 35:16-18.

As you read, use this chart to keep track of important details. Note how each mother fits into the narrative. It may be a completely foreign idea to you, but in Jacob's time, it was social normality in that culture for a woman's servant to act as her surrogate; the children born to such a servant were credited to the wife.

The birth order has been numbered for you, so fill in each son's name and the comment his mother made as she chose his name. For this study, we are only focusing on male children. The youngest has been filled in for you since his circumstances are a little different.

Leah	
1.	
2.	
3.	
4.	
9.	
10.	
Rachel	
11.	
12. Benjamin	Son of my right hand (Ben-Oni means son of my trouble)
Zilpah	
7.	
8.	
Bilhah	
5.	
6.	

Already, you can see this family is not without its share of drama! Tomorrow we will see that the drama is only getting started.

Week 1, Day 2

The Story of God from Genesis to Joshua Continued

	Details we learn for each brother	Blessings given by Israel to each son
Leah		
1. Reuben		
2. Simeon		
3. Levi		
4. Judah		
9. Issachar		
10. Zebulun		
Rachel		

11. Joseph		
Manasseh		
Ephraim		
12. Benjamin		
Zilpah		
7. Gad		
8. Asher		
Bilhah		
5. Dan		
6. Naphtali		

Today we are going to follow the story of the 12 sons of Israel. As we go through today's Scripture, use the middle column of the chart to note any details you learn about each man.

Young Joseph (Son number 11, born to Israel's beloved Rachel) was gifted with prophetic dreams and a big mouth. His father favored him, and he bragged about his dreams to his brothers. His brothers hated him for it.

Read Genesis 37:12-36. Remember to make notes in the chart above to help keep all of the players straight. As the baby of the family, Benjamin was most likely not a part of this event.

Today is jam-packed, but if you have the time, Genesis 38 includes an interesting story that will let you get to know Judah better.

Now, Joseph had been sold into slavery and landed in Egypt. He did some growing up, and he worked hard, winning the respect of his master, a prominent official. His master's wife took note that Joseph was "well-built and handsome," (Gen.19:6) and threw herself at him. She became enraged when Joseph refused and accused him of attacking her. Joseph's master had no choice but to throw him in jail. While in prison, God continued to bless Joseph with prophetic dreams, and though he was forgotten and left to rot for two years, God had not forgotten him.

Read Genesis 41:17-40

1.   **What would the next seven years be like in Egypt?**

2.   **What would happen in the seven years after that?**

3.   **What honor had been given to Joseph?**

The famine was so wide-spread that even Joseph's family was in need of food and his older brothers traveled to Egypt to beg for food. When they came face to face with Joseph, they did not recognize their brother.

Read Genesis 42:8-13.

4.   **Who was it the brothers said was "no more"?**

Read Genesis 42:14-38.

5.   Why do the brothers believe this difficulty has befallen them?

6.   How did the brothers describe Joseph in verse 33?

Some time passed, and the famine continued, and against Jacob's wishes, it became necessary to beg for food again. The full story is in Genesis 43-44. Joseph was understandably emotional when he saw his baby brother again.

7.   What was different about Joseph's relationship with Benjamin from all of his other brothers?

During this second meeting with his brothers, Joseph continued to hide his identity from them. He set up a ruse to keep Benjamin with him, but this time his brothers behaved like brothers.

Read Genesis 44:18-33.

8.   What do you think led to such a protective response from Judah?

Finally, Joseph reveals his identity to his brothers. He forgives them and invites them to remain in Egypt where they could live well during the time of famine. This reconciliation is a turning point in our narrative. The brothers, the sons of Israel, are finally unified, and in the same instant, they leave the Promised Land for comfort in Egypt.

9. In Genesis 45:17-20, who extended the generous invitation to Joseph's family?

Read Genesis 46:1-4

10. What is God's opinion of the move? What does he promise Israel?

Read Genesis 48.

In the chart above, use the last column to record the new details Israel's blessings reveal.

11. What significant decision does Israel make in verse 5?

12. What extra inheritance does Israel leave to Joseph in verse 22?

Read Genesis 49. Continue to record the details revealed in Israel's blessings on each of his sons.

13. What significant figure do we learn would come from Judah's line?

Look at Numbers 13:8, 16.

14. What significant figure will come from Joseph's line through Ephraim?

As God promised, He was with Israel, and for 400 years God did allow the descendants of Israel to multiply into a great nation.

After a few generations, their numbers threatened the Egyptians, who reacted by enslaving the Hebrews. Roughly 400 years into their time in Egypt, the Hebrews cried out to God to save them. God responded by calling Moses to be His prophet. God spoke directly to Moses and appointed Moses to lead the Hebrews. The Pharaoh of Egypt did not let his workforce go easily. God sent ten plagues on Egypt until Pharaoh finally let them go.

Soon after releasing the Hebrews, the Pharaoh decided to go after them and cornered the Hebrews at the Red Sea. The Hebrews faced the Egyptian army on one side or drowning on the other. But God intervened in the form of a pillar of fire between the Egyptians and Hebrews.

While holding off the enemy by fire, God caused the Red Sea to part, so the Hebrews could cross over on dry land. The pillar of fire lifted and the Egyptian army gave chase, but once the Hebrews had safely crossed, the water went back in place and the enemy was killed.

When we begin tomorrow, we meet the Hebrews being led in the wilderness by Moses and his assistant, Joshua. The Hebrews are organized by tribe, each named for the son of Israel from whom they descended: Reuben, Simeon, Levi, Judah, Dan, Naphtali, Gad, Asher, Issachar, Zebulun, Benjamin, and - in place of Joseph – Manasseh and Ephraim. You will notice that Scripture often refers to twelve tribes; the tribe of Levi (the Levites) were not counted among the rest of the Israelites. We will get a better look at that tomorrow and in week 6.

If you stuck with me, you have done a ton of work these first two days! We had to rush through a lot of information, but as we move along in this study, I think you will appreciate the history of the people we will get to know over the next few weeks. Join me tomorrow so I can introduce you to Joshua!

Week 1, Day 3

From the Highest High to the Lowest Low

I've spent a lot of time wondering when my time will come. When will my potential be fulfilled? When will I find success? When will people notice how humbly I've been working all along? (That last one is dripping with sarcastic irony!) I find myself simultaneously feeling like this journey, figuring out who I am and what I am supposed to do with my life, is taking forever, and I feel like I still have a lot of growing up left to do.

If you are already familiar with Joshua, you may think of him as a mighty military leader of Israel, which he did turn out to be. But digging into his story, I have found accounts of his younger years, while God was preparing him for his role as a leader, reveal a quiet disciple. He didn't hang out in the spotlight and didn't appear to seek glory or recognition. He soaked up wisdom and learned from his mentor, Moses. I have a lot to learn from Joshua!

Read Exodus 24:12-18

1. **If this is a familiar story to you, did you recall Joshua being with Moses on this trip up Mount Sinai?**

2. **Have you ever been part of something important, and had your name left out, or your participation overlooked? How did that feel at the time?**

3. **Does this glimpse of Joshua cast a different light on such experiences?**

I find some comfort in seeing that this servant of God was a quiet figure in his earlier years. He would have his time as a leader, but early on he was content to be near the leader, to be a student. Imagine what it would have felt like to be in Joshua's place in Exodus 24. Have you ever been invited so close to the Shekinah glory of God, the manifest presence of the Almighty? What an honor! Being in the presence of God changes our perspective. It takes the focus off of self and forces it where it belongs: on God.

4. **Think of a time when you have felt God's presence the most intensely. Share what that felt like, how you recognized it, and how it impacted you.**

Joshua and Moses spent a week on the mountain before Moses entered the cloud for forty days and nights. I'm not sure how Joshua spent those days. Did he help Moses in the cloud or, was he camped alone just outside? Either way, he had his own incredible experience away from the masses and close to God. He had a front row seat to one of the most significant moments in history. He saw God's power and glory and willingness to be intimate with His people.

During the forty days and nights, God gave Moses the details for building the Tabernacle and the Ark of the Covenant in great detail. He gave instructions for the Priesthood, offerings, and Sabbath.

The rest of the Hebrews did not expect Moses to be gone for so long. The way they handled their uncertainty was disappointing and very nearly brought on total destruction.

Read Exodus 32:1-20

Isn't this so often the way things go? Joshua had a literal mountaintop experience only to come down the mountain and find a catastrophe. While he immersed himself in the holiest of encounters, his fellow Hebrews were in chaos. Even Aaron (Moses' brother) had been swept up in the people's desire for something tangible to worship and was complicit in their idolatry.

5. **Can you think of a time you have returned from a mountaintop experience to find chaos? How did that impact your experience?**

One year I went to a Christian women's conference and felt filled to the brim, only to have to race home as my husband had an emergency appendectomy. He had complications from the anesthesia, and I sat in a hospital waiting room with my two young children. They were not allowed to go to the recovery room and were too young to leave alone, and I had no one I could call to help out – our family was out of state, and I hadn't made any close friends yet; we hadn't lived in our town for very long at that time. The holy high I'd had that morning was replaced by intense fear and loneliness. The truth of the matter is there were people who would have been there to help, but I didn't know how to ask for help; I felt like I would have been imposing. If you knew of any young mom in such a situation, would you hesitate to help? Of course not!

Why is it so hard to ask for help? If I had merely asked for it, my experience would have been much different. (In the end, my husband was fine, praise God!)

6. **Think back to your most recent time of needing help or support. Did you admit your need? Were people there to assist? If you didn't ask for help, how did that work out?**

Another mountain top to a crash moment in my life was work-related. I was feeling very inspired and excited about plans I had made, and when I took that excitement to my boss, I never even got to say a word about my plans. Instead, I encountered some criticism, and I let that go right to my core and send me into a depression. I let those dreams die.

7. **Can you relate? Have you ever let someone's negativity change your whole outlook on life?**

8. **If you could send a message to yourself in such a moment, what would you say?**

Read Exodus 32:26-29

9. **What group of people quickly claimed allegiance to the Lord?**

10. **What was the reward for their faithful devotion?**

How did Joshua respond to that crash after his mountaintop experience? Lucky for him, we have no idea! I hope as we mature in age and spiritual maturity, we get more graceful in our responses to post mountain top crashes! I know I am relieved not to have any video of my earliest crash reactions! What we do know is that somehow, Joshua stuck it out. He continued to learn under Moses, and became a great servant of the Lord's!

Week 1, Day 4

Faithful Spies

There have been moments in which I have been the lone optimist in a group, and others when I have scoffed at the optimist. So when I look at today's lesson and try to imagine which character I'd be, I can't be sure. I like to think I'd be one of the faithful few, but I know I am prone to being a complainer. I know God is powerful, but I am quick to forget that He would use that power for my benefit.

Read Numbers 13: 16-33

Notice in verse 16, Moses changed Hoshea's name to Joshua. The name Hoshea meant *salvation*, while Joshua (*Yehoshua* in the language of the time) means *Yahweh saves*. Several key servants of God experienced a name change to signify their relationship with God. Abram became Abraham, Sarai became Sarah, Simon became Peter, and Saul became Paul.

1. **Why do you think that detail is tucked into a single verse at this point in the narrative?**

I am a huge proponent of sharing what God does in your life as much as you can! Sharing such testimonies goes a long way in encouraging brothers and sisters in their faith journey! But sometimes, I sense God doing very personal things in my life. I don't feel able to share it in a way others would understand.

For Joshua to have his name changed must have been a significant moment to him. The name says a lot about his position. His name used to be "salvation" - almost as if, when his momma named him, she was announcing that he was God's gift to the people he would encounter. But the new name, "Yahweh saves," announces that salvation comes through God alone. Joshua would be an instrument, a tool in God's hands. That must have been a humbling honor. And scripture only gives us a tiny glimpse!

One of my most life-changing encounters with God happened several years ago. I don't think I've ever shared it out loud because of its personal nature and the fact that no words could do it justice. Since I am about to ask you to share of a time like that, I will do my best to put my experience into words.

I was on a planning team for my denomination's district children's camp, and each leader was going to give the message for a session. This opportunity would be my first time sharing a sermon I had written myself, and the largest group I had ever spoken in front of. I had been a witness to several children's sermons that had a significant impact on the kids and myself, so the bar had been set pretty high. A few hours before I was going to preach, I found a secluded spot on the campground. I had prayerfully done all of the preparation, but I needed it to be God speaking. I prayed for an anointing – and at that moment, I felt God's anointing presence in a way that shook me! I can't even think of words to do that feeling justice, but what I can say is that it was nothing natural, and it drove me into a posture of humility. I didn't want the moment to end!

2. **Can you think of moments God has had an impact on you and you weren't sure how to share that? Try to share it here!**

3. **What did the twelve spies find in the land of Canaan?**

List the positives …   List the negatives …

4. **In their place, do you think you would be more likely to react in fear of the fortified cities and giant soldiers, or to react in faith, raring to conquer the land in spite of those factors?**

Read Numbers 14.

5. **How did Joshua and Caleb respond when the people despaired over the reports of the faithless spies? (v.6-9)**

6. **What was the result of the people not having the faith to move forward into the Promised Land? (v.10-23)**

7. **What do you think the following 40 years were like for Joshua and Caleb?**

8. **Can you share a time when you had to go through the consequences for someone else's actions? What did you learn through that time?**

9. **What was promised to Joshua and Caleb that might have helped them persevere through the 40 years?** (v.24, 30)

I have to admit that trying to place myself in this narrative is uncomfortable. The people we've looked at over these first two days of study all came out of Egypt. According to Numbers 10:11, this was just over two years after leaving Egypt. So they remember what slavery felt like, they witnessed the plagues God brought on Egypt to set them free, they walked through the Red Sea on dry ground themselves, and they have witnessed countless miracles since then, not the least of which was the visible pillar of cloud by day and fire by night – the manifest presence of God!

In light of that, I truly hope I'd have been as faithful as Joshua and Caleb! But when I place myself in the role of one of the multitude hearing the reports of the ten faithless spies, I have a sad feeling that I would have been as shaken as they were.

10. **Can you think of a time you let someone else's negativity shake your faith? How do you wish you had responded? (How will you respond next time?)**

Next week we will move to the book of Joshua, at the end of these 40 years he has been waiting. He did a lot of growing up in that time and continued to study under his mentor, Moses. When we see him next, he's older, wiser, tougher, and ready for the next phase of the journey!

Week 1, Day 5

Life in the Wilderness Years

Because this study is centered on Israel finally entering and claiming the Promised Land, let's spend today looking at what life was like in the wilderness. When we read about the people finally setting their feet on the land God had promised them, I want to appreciate and share in their excitement!

At the end of Day Two, you read that the Hebrews were led by God's presence in the form of a pillar of cloud by day and a pillar of fire by night when they crossed through the Red Sea. That presence never left during the years in the wilderness.

Read Numbers 9:15-23

Take a moment to imagine what it was like there and then. Can you imagine such a cloud hovering over your car, or your workplace, or your home? There could be no clearer way to discern when God wants you to move on or stay put! Unfortunately, I have never seen such a clear visible indicator, at least not that I have recognized. We have to pray and do our best to discern God's will and direction.

1. **Imagine you are in the camp. Do you think that visible cloud would be comforting or frightening? Do you think you could go on with life as usual?**

I imagine I would be stunned. I picture myself staring with my jaw on the floor in total awe. But this was a constant presence for 40 years. Following this train of thought, I realize how awed I was when I first became aware of the Holy Spirit within me, guiding me. I mourn the realization that I have become so used to His presence that I can take it for granted and even forget about it.

2. **How do you think we can keep that sense of awe and reverence for God fresh?**

Let's move on to another aspect of life in the wilderness.

Read Exodus 16:1-31

How amazing it was of God to provide such reliable food! The people could count on it every single day, and though some of them tested the command to only take what they needed for each day, they learned that they could count on it showing up newly each morning without fail.

Read Numbers 11:1-6

3. **What are your thoughts on their romanticized comment about the food in Egypt having no cost?**

As the readers, we can see how absurd this complaining was! Slavery was an enormous cost for the food they ate in Egypt, and now they are not only free, but their food is provided daily at no cost at all - they didn't even have to work for it! How dare they complain? Aren't we guilty of the same?

4. What have you become bored with or sick of for which you should be giving thanks?

The time in the wilderness was not easy, but the people had the constant presence, provision, and protection of the Lord. They grumbled and complained, but they also learned to worship. We began this lesson with a look at the cloud hovering over the tabernacle. The tabernacle was constructed in the wilderness using plans given to Moses from God. It was designed to be set up and taken down as they traveled through the wilderness, and was the portable version of the temple they would one day build in Jerusalem. They did not wait to enter the Promised Land to begin living out the activities of their faith; God used the wilderness years to teach His people how to live in communion with Him.

He also used the years to train the fighting men of Israel. As they traveled, they came across adversarial groups and engaged in skirmishes, and God gave them numerous victories. I've marveled at the way I can look back over my own life and see how events or situations which seemed random or pointless at the time actually played big parts in preparing me for roles God would have for me.

5. If you look back now, what can you see that God has used to prepare you?

Read Numbers 21:32 and jot down the name of the city at the center of that skirmish.

Read Numbers 32:1-5

6. Which tribes approached the leaders?

7. What was their reason for making this request?

Read Numbers 32:6-15

Of course, Moses was immediately reminded of the ten faithless spies whose fear spread through the camp and led to 40 years of wandering through the wilderness until the faithless generation died off. We see that Moses definitely learned to be bold as he confronted these tribes.

Read Numbers 32: 16-28, and verse 33.

8. What agreement did these tribes and leaders make?

9. In verse 33, what group was included in this deal?

The tribe of Manasseh was especially large, and we will see in week five that half of the tribe settled east of the Jordan River and the other half settled west of the Jordan River. Often, Reuben, Gad, and the half tribe of Manasseh are referred to as the Trans-Jordan Tribes or, less formally, the two and a half tribes.

Week One Small Group Note Space

Discussion Questions

Day 1 – Chart

Day 2 – Chart, 6, 7, 8, 13, 14

Day 3 – 2, 3, 4, 8

Day 4 – 2, 7, 8

Day 5 – 2, 3, 4, 5

Use this space to record prayer requests and praises from the study group each week.

A Command With a Promise

Read Moses' words in Deuteronomy 1:37-38

1. **What was Moses to do for Joshua?**

There are a few special women who have made it their job to encourage me, and they are so good at it! I went far too long in my life, and then in my Christian walk without any encouragers, and it is a hard way to live. As a friend and I were complaining to each other about this problem a few years ago, we agreed to be encouragers to each other. We are at very similar places in our journey, so neither of us really qualifies to mentor the other, but just having that person to encourage me was a turning point.

2. **Do you have any people in your life who encourage you? Take a moment and send them a text or email, or – better yet! – a handwritten note to let them know how much that encouragement means. Share here how they encourage you.**

3. **Have you made it your mission to be an encourager to someone else? Take a moment to think of who is in your sphere of influence - someone you could adopt with this mission in mind. Put their name here as a commitment, and send them an encouraging word.**

That encouragement can be just a note or a well-timed meme or text saying something as simple as, "I prayed for you today, hope all is well!" Another option is to make it a rule to send something whenever that person comes to mind.

In Moses and Joshua's case, it became Moses' job to mentor Joshua. He needed to prepare Joshua to take the place of leadership. When the time came to pass the torch, Joshua had to have the respect of the people, confidence in himself, and a solid ability to hear and obey the Lord.

Read Deuteronomy 31:1-8

Write out verse 6 below!

Now, read Joshua 1: 1-9

Write out verse 9 below!

Don't you just love how consistent God's message is? As we read through the book of Joshua, you will see the words, "Be strong and courageous," "Do not fear," and, "Do not be afraid" repeated over and over. If you write in your Bible, choose a way to mark that phrase, or any variation of that phrase, each time you come to it.

Now read verse 9 one more time. The Lord told Joshua this is His command.

4. **What is significant about a command, as opposed to a statement?**

5. **Now go deeper. Would God give us a command we are not capable of obeying?**

I don't know where you landed on that last question, but I believe if God commands something, we must be capable. That doesn't mean it is easy, or even fast, but I believe we have the ability to be strong and courageous. And, oh, do I feel more capable some days than others.

So we can be strong and courageous but how? Read the rest of verse 9.

6. **What reason does God give for us not to be afraid or discouraged?**

That is a promise, my friend! Your God will be with you wherever you go! That knowledge does something for me. It lets me feel like my feet are planted on solid ground.

7. **What are you facing that would be easier with the knowledge that the Lord your God goes before you and with you?**

I've had plenty of fear in my life. I grew up as the daughter of American diplomats living overseas. As kids, we were trained, on a regular basis, to be alert for typical kidnapping tactics. We were high-risk targets. At age 9, I would walk home from the bus stop watching for vans with no windows, ready to sprint in a zig-zag pattern. I knew where the soft parts were to pinch and claw at an attacker if I were grabbed (eyes, throat, underarms, etc.)

For a few years, I lived in Denmark in a house that was very old and had a cellar. It was a rental, so the owners had part of the cellar closed off by what appeared to be prison bars. There were no lights, so I imagined all kinds of creepy things there. It was while living there that I discovered scary novels and developed a paralyzing fear of death. I didn't understand what happened to a person when they died, and I imagined the worst. I was certain there were zombies in that cellar prison!

As a young mom, I found myself experiencing the most intense fear of my life when my baby was sick and needed to be hospitalized for dehydration, and again, when he was a young boy and anaphylaxis caused him to stop breathing as we drove to the ER. (Thankfully he is fine!)

Fear can take so many shapes. It can be logical or not. There can be a cause or not. My fear when a suspicious man approaches is understandable – it alerts me to possible danger, and prompts me to action. My fear of taking a cruise is much less reasonable. I have never had a bad experience on the water, but the idea of not being able to swim to land keeps me from even considering taking a cruise someday.

8.   What are some areas where fear has a grip on your life?

9.   What are your thoughts on these fears in light of Joshua 1:9?

Surround Yourself With People Who Will Affirm God's Promises and Commands

Whew! Yesterday, we opened up a can of worms, talking about our fears. That's going to keep coming up in this study because Joshua is full of lessons on dealing with fear. I want to linger here a bit longer. God commands us to be strong and courageous, and in the same breath He says, "*because* the Lord your God will be with you wherever you go." What a promise to cling to!

Today, read all of Joshua 1. (It's okay, it's only 18 verses!)

1. **What was the first bit of advice God gave Joshua, which he was to pass on to the Israelites and us? (v. 7,8)**

2. **What special deal had been made with the Reubenites, Gadites, and half-tribe of Manasseh? (v.12-15)**

Those groups had chosen to settle east of the Jordan River. God allowed that decision. But the fighting men of those tribes were still required to help the whole nation of Israel take possession of the Promised Land, which was west of the Jordan. (Numbers 32)

3. **Sum up the response they give Joshua. (v. 16-18)**

4. **Write out that last sentence they say to Joshua in verse 18!**

They repeat that beautiful command back to Joshua! Be strong and courageous!

I told you Joshua was full of lessons for dealing with fear, and this is one of them. We need to surround ourselves with people who will repeat and remind us of God's promises and commands. This lesson is such an important part of living a faithful life; if the people whom we listen to the most are not believers, or make fun of what we believe, it is infinitely more difficult to live a life that pleases Jesus.

Does that mean we cut the non-believers out of our lives? Of course not! What it means is that we need to make sure the people who have the most influence over us are the ones we want to be influenced by.

5. **Take a moment to assess your relationships. Who are the people who have the most influence on you?**

If you find that you are short on positive, Christ-honoring people in your inner circle, this Bible study is a great time to change that! If you are doing this study in a group, the people in your group are probably good candidates to start building relationships with. If you have a church you attend, pick out some people you'd like to get to know. If you are new to this whole church thing, I highly recommend you do something that will sound crazy – peek around for someone who seems like they know what's going on and ask them to help you learn.

If you are not so new to this whole church thing, look out for those who are! Would you give someone your phone number, friend them on social media, make a point of including them? When I was a new Christian, I was also an introvert (still am!) and was not about to reach out to ask for help. I made it so hard on myself. Unfortunately, my struggles went unnoticed by those with more experience than myself; I faked being fine, so no one knew to offer help.

6. Do you feel like God has made any promises to you? Has He called you to something? Share in the space below.

Early in my Christian walk, before I had any idea that God would whisper directly to my spirit, I felt like God had put a huge plan in my head. I had been a hairdresser and a very poor, young mother. I had a vision of a salon which would provide on-site childcare for mothers in similar positions to my own, and would also provide free services to unemployed people to help them prepare for interviews. It could have been such an incredible ministry! But I didn't tell a soul about it. I thought it was too big. Then I allowed my license to expire because, in the panic of financial troubles, I thought it was too expensive to renew.

Looking back, I can see how I hindered the plan. I made a friend at my new church, she was ten years older than me, and she was a hairdresser. Had I opened up, she would have advised that letting my cosmetology license expire would be a costly mistake. She could have connected me with people who could have made that dream a reality. Now, I keep hearing of ministries like the one I dreamed of and I wish I had shared it years ago so someone could have helped me follow it.

Fast forward a few years and God has called me to preach! I began taking ministerial classes and made a dear friend. Since then we have pushed each other along the way. We keep each other accountable. She learned quickly, in a classroom setting, that I love to write. I've said several times that I feel called to write a Bible study, and she keeps reminding me of it.

Finally, several months ago, I began studying Joshua as I was preparing a message for a women's conference and told her I was sure I needed to write a study on Joshua. She kept bringing that back up to me. Finally, a few weeks ago, when I was complaining that I felt like I had no sense of direction, she said, "Hey, didn't God tell you to write that Bible study? Pen to paper, sister." Later that day, I began the outlining process.

7. **Look back at the last question. With whom will you share those promises?**

Whether it is the promises and commands made to all believers through Scripture, or promises and commands God has given to you personally, make sure to surround yourself with people that will affirm those in your life! When distraction or fear threaten to knock you off course, those people are a remarkable source of strength and courage.

When Plans Go Off the Rails

Read Joshua 2:1-3

Do you think Joshua only sent in two spies because, in his experience, only two spies were faithful? I joke, but I think his years of experience did have an impact here. The spies went into Jericho on a recon mission. Joshua knew that Jericho was the next city they were to conquer, but he had no idea yet how the victory would be won. So he proceeded to take the actions his military training told him were the wise ones, ever ready for God to step in with new instructions.

The spies who went into Jericho were trustworthy and capable. They knew the promises God had made, and they knew that when they acted according to God's commands, victory was always theirs.

1. **So what would be going through your head if you found yourself where they did in the verses you just read?**

2. **Can you think of a time you were doing everything right, to the best of your knowledge and ability, and everything went wrong? What questions were you asking in that situation?**

Read Genesis 18:20-33, 19:12-13

Following Abraham's conversation with the Lord, Sodom and Gomorrah were, indeed, destroyed. So there were not even ten righteous people found in those cities. Lot did live there, and we see that while God did not spare the city for Lot's sake, *Lot* was spared!

Now in Joshua 2, Jericho faces destruction, and the spies just so happened to find themselves in Rahab's home when they needed to hide.

3. **Do you think the plan had been derailed or was this God's plan all along?**

4. **Share a time when things seemed to go wrong and God used it to bring about something even better than you expected.**

Read Joshua 2:4-11

For the longest time, when I read this account in Scripture, I thought this was God using Rahab to put the plan back on track, that Rahab had been in the right place at the right time. Now I think this was His plan all along. Rahab didn't save the mission; she *was* the mission!

Rahab told the spies that all of Jericho had heard of the victories God had given the Hebrews. She says their hearts were melting in fear.

5. Can you think of a time you would describe your heart as melting with fear?

Rahab also tells the spies that she knows the Lord has already given the land into their hands. While they were likely wondering if they had heard God wrong or if God had changed His mind, this stranger to them, a prostitute of Jericho, repeated God's promise to them. She probably had no idea of the significance of her words and yet, what a reassurance they must have been!

Often, God uses the words of others, a song at just the right time, the right phrasing in your daily Scripture reading or Bible study, or other little ways to reassure us that He is in control and He has not forgotten us.

6. Share a time when you have known this to be true.

Read Proverbs 3:5-6, Proverbs 16:1-4, Proverbs 16:9, 2 Peter 3:9

We can't know all of God's plans, and He only reveals to us what we need to know when we need to know it. But, what do we know for certain about His plans based on those verses?

Week 2, Day 4

Let Your Fear Drive You TO God

Read Joshua 2: 12-20

Rahab's fear drove her to God! She knew that the God who helped the Hebrews was powerful, and she wanted to be counted among those whom His power protected. She knew something about the Lord before the spies showed up at her house. She knew her city would soon fall to Israel, and she had every reason to melt in fear at the coming war. Can you imagine what went through her mind when her door burst open and two Hebrew men entered seeking safety? Her instinct was to protect them, and she did so *before* striking any deal for her own protection.

But strike a deal, she did! She secured her safety and the safety of her household. In a moment of desperation, Rahab kept a level head and took action to protect herself and her family. Oh, how I want to be a woman like that!

I am amazed at how level headed I can be in some situations, and how quickly I lose my ever-loving mind in others! When I was a senior in high school, my friend and I were having lunch at a fast food restaurant after school. As I often do, I was staring out the window while we were talking, so I saw as the delivery man was walking down the ramp from his truck with a dolly loaded with boxes and suddenly went down. I could see that his leg had gone through the grated metal ramp. I yelled for someone to call 9-1-1, and ran out the door to help.

The man was much bigger than I was and I had no medical training beyond the first aid training we had taken in health class. I don't know what I thought I was doing, but I ran to the emergency. This poor man had metal through his leg. I will spare you from the details, except to say that this was a gory scene. Somehow, I, as an 18-year-old girl, convinced the man not to try to pull his leg free on his own, and I kept the scene calm until the professionals arrived.

As a mom, I have had lots of moments when I faced emergencies with an unearthly calm, similar to that day. But then there are moments when I have not a lick of sense or calm when I face the unexpected!

One day my sweet golden retriever, Buster, hopped the fence into my neighbor's yard and caught a squirrel. He hopped back into my yard shaking the poor critter like a toy. I ran back into the house screaming! I called my husband at work and insisted he come home and deal with the murder dog! My husband, of course, could not leave work for something so trivial ("Trivial? Didn't you hear me say *murder dog*?!"), so I cried and left Buster in the yard for hours while I waited until my husband came home to deal with it. Where was my level head that day?

1.   **Share a time when you let panic drive your actions.**

2.   **Share a time when you were calm when many people would typically panic.**

3.   **Which response yields better results? Why do you think that is?**

Science tells us that every creature has a natural response to fear; fight, flight, or freeze. It is a built-in alarm system. God built that alarm system to alert us to danger. If you watch nature shows, you'll see animals that do any of those three things as their survival instincts kick in. I especially get a kick out of the poor fainting goats that become paralyzed when they are scared. I wonder how that works for survival - perhaps the predator laughs too hard to eat them!

As I thought about these fear responses, I realized that the same descriptions apply to long term fears - such as fear of the future, for our kids, over finances, the list goes on. What do those look like in real life?

Fight: Irritability, always being on the offensive, looking for the next fight or cause for offense.

Flight: Avoiding people, avoiding conflict, avoiding the outside world, literally running away or leaving.

Freeze: Having no idea what to do, so doing nothing at all and being too afraid to take any action. You are paralyzed by fear. It is comical when it's a goat in a field in no real danger, but not nearly so funny to experience.

Our minds associate fear with certain conditions we have experienced as dangerous so that the next time we face similar conditions, internal alarms go off as a warning. Perhaps it is a sound, or a particular face, or any number of triggers. In its most extreme, this is what happens for people who suffer from Post-Traumatic Stress; certain conditions strongly remind them of danger, and their brain sends their body signals to brace for danger.

Sometimes the fear signals are needless. That crash in the dark was just the wind knocking something over. Other times that crash in the dark could be an intruder. Sometimes the noise in the dark parking lot is just a stray cat wandering through. Other times the noise is someone with evil plans from whom we should run. The fear response is there for a purpose.

Yet with all of this evidence that God created a fear response within us, God says so many times in scripture that we should not be afraid. I think the real directive, here, is that **we should not *remain* in a state of fear**! When the alarm goes off, we need to pay attention. Look around and assess the situation. If there is a problem or danger, we should take action.

4.   What did Rahab do with her fear?

5.   Look back to Joshua 2:9-11. What did the rest of Jericho do with their fear?

The rest of Jericho shared Rahab's fear, but their response was not the same. They set themselves against God. They were too afraid to march on Israel in battle, but they were cowering, and preparing for war to come to them - they were not about to submit to God's authority. Spoiler alert: they made the wrong choice.

When something triggers our fear response, we have a choice to make. How will we respond to it? Will we set ourselves against God, as Jericho did, or run to Him, as Rahab did?

It's easy to recognize a quick fear response when someone jumps out at you, or there is an apparent moment of fright. But take some time to think about those long-term fears. I've heard from many women who came into situations with a sense of fear they didn't even realize they had.

6.   How can we recognize fear has taken root in those less obvious situations?

7.   Has today's study alerted you to any fear currently gripping you? If so, what will you do with it?

The Best Time to Take Action

Read Joshua 2:21-24

1. **When did Rahab place the red cord out the window?**

Look back at verse 16. The spies were to hide in the hills for three days before heading back to their camp. The journey back probably took at least a few days, and then more time would pass before Israel marched to Jericho. She had plenty of time to act, but she chose to do so immediately.

2. **Why do you think Rahab didn't wait to place the cord out the window?**

So many thoughts come to mind for me. For one thing, I like to take action when I am facing a problem. If there is something I can do to make things better, I want to do so. If there isn't something to do, I tend to find something to keep me busy instead. Once in a while, that manifests in meticulous house cleaning, but not nearly often enough! More than that, though, taking a step of faith combats the fear. It forces you to move forward! Hanging that cord from the window said, "No turning back now!" It was an action which cemented her decision to follow God.

3. Have you ever decided to be faithful, only to forget about it, get distracted, or talk yourself out of it?

I have done that more times than I can count! This Bible study is coming about, in part, thanks to this lesson I learned from Rahab. I knew I would be likely to talk myself out of it or get distracted with something else, so I hung the scarlet cord out the window by telling my accountability partner and my Sunday School class that I am writing it. Once I said it out loud, I had to follow through!

Read Psalm 119:60, John 13:17, James 4:17

4. What do these verses tell you about the importance of acting in faith?

In Esther 4, Mordecai has learned of a plot to kill all of the Jews, and asks his niece, Queen Esther, to approach the king to request his intervention to save them. She responds in fear, knowing that to approach the king uninvited could mean certain death.

Read Esther 4: 12-17

Esther was terrified, as any sensible woman in her place would have been, but she did act in faith. Notice something about her situation: she needed a push! I do too, more often than I'd like to admit!

5. Whom can you trust to push you to act in faith when you'd much rather chicken out?

Read 1 Samuel 17:1-7, 32-37

This story comes to mind when I think of having faith like a child. Young David didn't even seem to recognize that there should be some fear of danger in the fight he was taking on!

6. **Can you think of a time when you moved in faith right away, without even considering alternatives?**

Read Jonah 1:1-4

Here's an example of a man doing just the opposite of what God told him to do. Running from God didn't work out for Jonah.

7. **Can you share a time when your actions moved you away from God's plan, and how that played out?**

I have fought God's plans at times. I am tremendously grateful for a handful of people in my life who will push me to act on faith when I am wavering. However, what I really want to be is a woman who, like Rahab and David, have the instinct to act on faith as a reflex action immediately.

Week Two Small Group Note Space

Discussion Questions:

Day 1 – 2, 4, 7, 9

Day 2 – 5, 6

Day 3 – 2, 3, 4, 6

Day 4 – 1, 2, 6, 7

Day 5 – 3, 4, 6, 7

Use this space to record prayer requests and praises from the study group each week.

Crossing the Jordan River

Have you been thinking about acting in faith since yesterday's lesson? Today's step of faith is an exciting one!

Read Joshua 3:1-5

Something big is about to take place; crossing into the Promised Land has been the most anticipated event of the past forty plus years! As it is right around the corner, Joshua instructs the people to consecrate themselves. Consecrating meant they were to set themselves aside as belonging to God.

Read Exodus 19:9-11, 14-15

1. **What physical actions did they take to display this consecration?**

Consecration brings the sacrament of baptism to mind. The act of being dunked in the water is not in and of itself consecrating, but when done as a declaration of the old self, being dead to sin and the believer rising in new life with Christ, it is a beautiful picture of setting oneself aside as belonging to God. But as believers, we are always to be set aside for Christ, so the act of consecrating ourselves to God should be ongoing.

2. **What are some things you can do when you sense the need to consecrate yourself?**

3. **Can you think of times when you have consecrated yourself, or times it may be necessary down the road?**

In my final year before becoming ordained, I took a Spiritual Formation class. One of my assignments - my favorite! - was to take a 24-hour retreat. I was to be completely secluded from other people; it was time for me to be alone with God. I chose to rent a hotel room not far from home. I brought my Bible, a journal, a playlist full of worship music, and prepared to hear from God. It isn't the sort of thing I can afford to do often, but that 24-hour retreat was amazing! I felt ready for my ordination after spending such intense time in prayer and worship with no distractions. If you can ever take a retreat like that, I highly recommend it! Especially if you have a big decision or potential life-changing event on the horizon! It allows you to cut out all other distractions and be sure that you are lined up with God's will.

I have found a more routine way of consecrating myself through observing the Lenten season. I discovered that forty days of fasting from something, plus adding specific actions to my days, drew me closer to God. While drawing closer to Him, we consequently set ourselves aside from the world. When I feel the need to set myself aside, I set a time frame for myself and abstain from something (usually something like caffeine or sugar) and add daily actions (something like requiring my time in the Word before I can pick up my phone at all, or some other spiritual discipline).

I have found the need for such things when something big is looming, but also when I find myself having drawn away from the Lord at all (usually because life got busy without me noticing), or when I find myself under spiritual attack. That sounds scary, but sometimes you can sense the enemy doing all he can to knock you down. These are times we need to be intentional about declaring that we belong to God, and taking action helps to cement that.

As I mentioned before, this act of consecrating ourselves should be ongoing, and that means we should be intentional about this daily as well. You may choose to start every morning with prayer and time reading Scripture. You may choose to listen to worship music throughout your day. Whatever it is, we would be wise to find ways of setting ourselves aside for God every day. We also need to be aware of the potential trap of routine; it is easy to allow yourself to go through the motions without genuinely engaging.

With that in mind, let's keep going!

Read Joshua 3:6-13

4.   When would the waters of the Jordan stop flowing?

Read Joshua 3:14-16

5.   What did we just learn about the condition of the Jordan?

Have you ever seen a river at flood stage? Recently, we had what felt like never ending rain. Almost every day it rained, it was dreary for ages. My husband and I went to see the river when we knew it had reached impressive flood stage depths. We stood on a bridge over the water, and it raced by, just a few feet below us. The water was far wider than usual, and there was debris crashing past. The water roared loud enough that we had to raise our voices, and my heart beat a bit faster even though I knew I was safe on the solid bridge.

Now imagine you are one of those priests who had to step into such a river. God promised the water would stop, but only *after* you stepped into it. Yikes! But God was true to His word, as He always is.

Sometimes God asks the same of us with the same promise.

Sometimes we have to take a step of faith while the circumstances around us are still terrifying. We have to take that first frightening step before we can see God's hand at work.

6. **Can you think of a time you took a step of faith when it didn't make sense, or your circumstances were treacherous? How did God respond to that step of faith?**

When we allow God to direct our steps, it is never as dangerous as it looks! When He promises safety and protection, He delivers!

I feel the need to throw a word of caution in here. Obedience is key in this lesson. Had the Israelites stepped into the flooded Jordan River without God's direction and protection, it would have been disastrously dangerous. When a step of faith would be hazardous without God's help, it needs to be steeped in prayer first to discern whether it is God's idea or your own.

7. **In the past, how have you been able to discern when something was God's direction as opposed to your own idea?**

If this is a new concept to you, or you just aren't sure, this is where other believers are so helpful. Find someone you trust and talk things through with them. One thing I can promise you: God never contradicts Himself, so the first test is to see whether it aligns with Scripture.

8. **Looking at the example in today's reading, what are your thoughts on taking a step of faith in scary circumstances?**

Week 3, Day 2

The Value of Mentors

Read Joshua 3:17

I just love this! The multitude of Israel was huge - far too big for everyone to see the miracle of the water stopping at the first step the priests took. So God instructed those priests, holding the Ark of the Covenant, to stand in the middle of that dry river bed as everyone else crossed through. That ark was a big deal. It was where the people knew the presence of God to dwell. So as the people who hadn't seen the miracle approached the dry river bed, they saw those priests and the holy presence of God and knew it was safe to keep going. When you haven't had the benefit of seeing the miracle for yourself, follow someone who has!

1. **Share an example of someone more mature in their faith or further along the road who encouraged you to keep going.**

Perhaps it was a job or career that is new to you, or a new phase of life, or marriage, or divorce, or grief, or a new hobby, or any number of things. Right now, I am leaning on some Navy wives and moms as I am new to being a Navy mom. My son will graduate high school in a month, and at the end of this summer, he ships off for boot camp. That is new and scary, and I need those who have gone ahead to help me out.

2. **What experiences have you had that you can draw from that could help someone else?**

Please know that you do not have to be an expert to share your knowledge and encouragement. Your feelings and experiences along the way can be more helpful than you can imagine. Sometimes the most encouraging thing to the person at the start of a road is simply knowing it is survivable and that someone has been where they are now. With that in mind, go back and add to the space above! You have more to share than you might think!

3. **Read the following verses and jot down what you learn about mentoring.**

Proverbs 1:5, Proverbs 27:17, Titus 2:2-8

Read Exodus 18:14-26

This passage is just one example of mentoring in action. Jethro, Moses' father-in-law, was older and experienced in leadership. Moses needed to learn something about delegation, but he didn't even know it. Jethro, in his experience, could see what Moses could not and he gave sage advice. Moses, to his credit, saw the advice as wise and put it into practice. It led to things being better for Moses and the people - this new system was far more productive, and Moses would be able to focus on things only he could do.

We're going to take a quick trip down a rabbit trail here because I can't be the only one who needs to look at this!

4. **What are the things you do yourself that only you can do?**

5. **What are the things you do yourself that could easily be done by someone else?**

Now let's get back on track; we were talking about following those who have had the benefit of seeing the miracle.

Read 1 Samuel 3:1-11

Eli was a prophet who was familiar with hearing the voice of God. Samuel was young, and when he heard the voice of God for the first time, he was confused. Eli's knowledge steered Samuel in the right direction.

Scripture is full of examples of God's servants mentoring others. So often I hear my peers, and people older than myself remarking on how troubled the next generation is, how much they don't know, how disrespectful they are, or any number of negative comments. If you've found yourself saying or thinking about such things, I have a hard question for you. What are you doing about it?

If we are going to have the honor and privilege of having a positive impact on the generation behind us, we have to have relationships with them. We have to spend time together, learn what matters to them, what they are involved in, how they think. We have to earn the right to speak into their lives. Once you get to know someone on that level, it is tough to make a blanket statement about them.

6. **Take a moment and think of who God might want you to begin building such a relationship with. Think about who He might have you mentor, and who He would have you follow.**

Week 3, Day 3

Remember All That The Lord Has Done

I am in the perfect place to write today's study, friend! Once a year, for the past ten years, I have made an annual trip to the mountains of Tennessee for a women's conference. The first two years were with a church group, but since the second year, my mother-in-law and sister-in-law have joined me. This year is my daughter's sixth year as part of the crew!

I look forward to this trip all year long for two reasons. One: it is always a great time with family, and two: God always shows up and speaks to me through this conference.

Something I couldn't share with you precisely, though, is what God has done each time. I have never taken the time to journal about it. It's usually earth-shaking to me, and I feel – in the moment – as if I could never forget. But time is funny like that. All I have is the general sense that God did something in my heart each year.

Read Joshua 4:1-9

1. What was the purpose of the memorial Joshua had them build?

Can we get personal? I want to talk about tattoos, and I know that talk can get testy in a church group. For the sake of not getting bogged down, let's get the potential drama out of the way by looking at biblical context. The tiny portion of scripture which warns against tattoos was written in a time when tattoos were not decoration; they were more like a brand declaring which false god a person was devoted to. In that context, the problem with tattoos is obvious. Today that isn't so much the case. Today, each tattoo has to speak for itself. I'll say that I love my husband's wedding ring tattoo (he works with vehicles and would prefer not to lose a finger thanks to machinery catching his ring!). But I'll be honest and say I judged the door-to-door salesman who showed up at my home displaying several tattoos of naked breasts in front of my child. (Yes, it is wrong to judge; I'm sorry!)

2. Now that we have that out of the way, do you have (or does a loved one have) a tattoo with special significance? Or, if you're like me, what meaningful tattoo would you have if you were not too scared of the pain? Write about that here.

A sweet friend has a beautiful tattoo as a memorial to her mother, whose loss to cancer she grieves. Another dear friend has a cute purple sneaker tattooed on her ankle to represent her bond with her sister. My sister has the word "breathe" on her wrist as a constant reminder that she has victory over anxiety. A precious mom has one of the neatest tattoos I have ever seen; if you look at it from one direction, it says "Buddy," and from the opposite, it says "Brady." That was the name of her son, who they affectionately called "Buddy". He died from a brain tumor, and this sweet woman cherishes any opportunity to talk about her son! I could go on and on. I also have a handful of friends with tattoos which remind them of who they were pre-Jesus. Those are some interesting conversation starters! They come with a testimony of a life changed!

3. **Now, take a mental walk through your home and garden. What pictures or statues or other memorial items do you have with the purpose of remembering a person or event?**

My sister has one of my favorites! She had her wedding bouquet dried and flattened in a frame on her wall. You can't look at that without remembering the day! In my kitchen windowsill, I have a little toy dragon – every time I look at it I remember and pray for the little girl who gave it to me; she was one of the children I ministered to a handful of years ago, one of those special kids who you have to love and claim as your own forever.

Again, I could go on for a long time on this topic, but you have other things to do today!

Here's the point. We don't build altars any more in today's culture, but we are really familiar with putting things which remind us of something in particular in our frequent line of sight. We hope that people will ask about the significance so we can share the story!

4. **Take another imaginary tour of your home and garden. What visual reminders do you have of things God has done for you?**

If you're anything like me, you wish you could think of more things, because He has certainly done a lot! I have thought about this a lot over recent years, and I might be ready to act on it now. I want more reminders of specific things the Lord has done to be placed all around my home. I've also frequently thought about tattooing certain verses or phrases on myself with that same purpose. However, I would be covered from head to toe if I did that, and so far I'm too afraid of the pain to have a single one!

Look back at today's scripture.

5. **What has just happened that they want to remember?**

6. **What is significant about where and when they built this memorial?**

7. **What major event is next on their agenda? (If your Bible has handy section titles, look near the end of chapter 5)**

Here's the lesson: *remembering all that the Lord has done will help us to face what is coming next!*

8. **The last thing I ask of you today: What are some significant things the Lord has done for you that you need to remember when you are facing future difficulties?**

We're going to go a little deeper with this tomorrow, so between now and then, be thinking about all that the Lord has done for you!

Week 3, Day 4

Memorial Moments in Scripture

Yesterday, Israel took the time to remember what the Lord had done. Today, we're going to poke around the rest of Scripture for more memorial moments.

Read Esther 9:20-23

In case you are unfamiliar with "these events" which Mordecai wanted everyone to remember annually, I'll give you the short version. (But if you can make time, the whole book can be read in one sitting, and it reads like a novel!)

Esther was a Jew living in captivity under the rule of King Xerxes. She became his top ranking wife but was subject to customs which forbade her to approach the King uninvited. An awful, high-ranking man named Haman became angry with Esther's uncle, Mordecai, when Mordecai refused to bow to him (bowing being reserved for God). Haman focused his anger into hatred of Mordecai and all Jews and tricked the King into signing an edict which would exterminate the Jews. Mordecai asked Esther to approach the King to plead with him to revoke the edict. Though terrified, she did approach her husband who received her generously and provided a loophole to the edict which would allow the Jews to live. Now, there is a Hollywood worthy twist for the evil Haman, but you'll have to read it for yourself!

So the festival of Purim became an annual memorial of God's protection through his servant, Esther.

Read Exodus 28:29-30

1. **What did this memorial do for Aaron as he carried out his priestly duties?**

This story makes me think of the weighty responsibility we volunteer for when we say we will pray for someone. I have learned that I have to stop and pray right when I say I will, or I am likely to become an accidental liar when I get busy and forget. There are situations where I commit to ongoing prayer for people, and I can easily forget then as well. I'm working on getting better at this. Some things I have done are setting a reminder on my phone, placing a picture of the person where I will see it frequently and be reminded to pray, committing that every time I do something in particular like every time I get in my car, I'll use it as a reminder to pray. With my son heading off to boot camp soon, I have given out dog tags or anchor charms to friends and family to serve as a reminder to pray for him.

2. **What are more practical things we can do to help us remember the ones we have chosen to be responsible for, as Aaron was for so many people?**

Read Genesis 28:10-22

3. **What was Jacob making a memorial to?**

4. **Do you have photos or tokens of some sort to remember major turning points in your own faith journey?**

5. **Are there songs or verses that you associate with significant God moments in your life?**

I tend to associate songs with important moments in my own life. The first worship song I heard after I gave my heart to Jesus brings that moment fresh to my mind any time I hear it. The song that led me to give God full control over my life almost always brings tears to my eyes as it helps me relive that moment. The hymn, Take My Life and Let it Be was my prayer during the months leading to my ordination service, and it was played during that service. It had such an impact on me that I wrote the lyrics on the inside cover of my Bible, and each time I see it or hear the song, I make that commitment again.

Memorials, whatever form they take, can enrich our Christian walk, they can help us to be more aware of what God has done and is doing in our lives.

Next week we will see God direct His people to celebrate the Passover each year as a memorial to remember how He rescued them from Egypt. That was a series of miracles, a display of His love that each following generation would need to be told about. That is the memorial meal Jesus was sharing with His disciples in the next memorial moment we're going to look at.

Read Luke 22:7-20, and 1 Corinthians 11:22-26

While observing one memorial of God saving His people from physical slavery, Jesus gave us a new memorial, the sacrament of the Lord's Supper (Communion) to help us remember God saving us from spiritual slavery.

6. **Why do you think Jesus said He eagerly desired to eat this Passover with His closest disciples?**

7. What did Jesus do with the cup, and what did He say?

8. What did Jesus do with the bread, and what did He say?

Something interesting about the four Gospels is that they differ in little ways. Any time multiple people witness the same event, it is normal for their recollection to differ, whether from different perspectives, different details mattering to them, or time elapsed since the event.

Read Matthew 26:26-29, and Mark 14:22-26.

9. Do any details stand out to you?

Matthew's account uses the phrase, "This is my blood of the covenant."

Read Exodus 24:4-11

10. What phrase did Moses use to describe the blood he used in the sacrifice?

11. Who did the elders see? (It is significant that they were allowed to see and not die!)

12. What did they do together?

Looking at these Scriptures side by side has me unbelievably excited! In Moses' story and at the Last Supper, select servants of the Lord were invited into the very presence of God. They were allowed to see Him and live, they partook in the salvation offered by the blood of the covenant, and they shared food and drink.

To eat and drink is something most of us do so often, we can do it without even thinking about it. It's a common daily occurrence. Friend, God wants to be with us in the mundane! Not only that, but He can give the mundane more significance! He longs for us to invite Him into every part of our lives.

The blood of the covenant Moses used in sacrifice was only enough to cover a certain amount of sin. It was an action that had to be taken over and over again and was never enough. The blood of the covenant that Jesus spilled was the sacrificial offering that *was* enough to cover all sins once and for all. It is a gift He offers freely. We need only to accept it. When believers partake in communion, we remember the cost, and we celebrate the gift that Jesus Christ gave us.

13. Close today by reflecting on the memorials we have looked at, and how they can enrich your life. Jot down anything that stands out to you.

God WAS Faithful at the Red Sea! God IS Faithful in the Jordan River! God WILL BE Faithful When You Face Jericho!

Read Joshua 4:10-13

1. Who had the Lord given his instructions through?

I think it's beautiful that even though Moses was not allowed to enter the Promised Land, God still allowed him to be such an integral part of the monumental moment. It makes my mom-heart extra tender toward God.

2. **If you're a parent, have you ever had to discipline your child in a way that absolutely broke your heart for them? Or if you are not a parent, can you think of a time your punishment might have been really hard for your parent to carry out?**

3. **What do we learn about the pace at which the people passed through the Jordan River?**

I wonder whether it was excitement or fear that caused them to hurry. Or, perhaps they hurried to shorten how long the priests would have to carry that heavy ark. It may have been some combination. I can think of many circumstances in which I have been assured that something is safe, but I still feel the need to rush the experience just in case. The water will not come rushing back, God is holding it back, and at no point is there any chance He will fatigue or get bored or distracted. Still, they hurried. Just in case?

I don't want to pick on the Israelites, mainly because I share their faults. I know God is bigger and better and able to do more than I could ask or imagine, and yet I spend countless hours trying to find my own solutions and back-up plans for things I say I am trusting Him for. And here's the tricky part of that: when it's happening, I believe that I do trust Him at the same time I am making back-up plans!

4. **Is this bringing to mind any areas where your worrying and fretting is a signal that you might not be trusting God as much as you could?**

If that brought some things up for you, take some time to pray about those areas. Ask God to increase your ability to trust Him and when you catch yourself worrying and fretting, be intentional about stopping that and going to prayer.

Read Joshua 4: 14

5. We know that God doesn't want us to worship anyone besides Him. Why do you suppose He chose to exalt Joshua in this way?

Read Joshua 4: 15-24

This passage is where I want to camp for a little while. Yesterday we looked at the importance of remembering all that the Lord has done. When we are facing something frightening or intimidating, it is such a gift to be able to look back at what God has already brought you through!

In verse 23 - I love this so much! - Joshua says, "The Lord your God did to the Jordan what He had done to the Red Sea." God's character is unlike any other we know. People change all the time, for better or worse. Our moods change. Our preferences change. Our abilities change. Experiences change us but not so with God. His character is unchanging. God was faithful yesterday, He is faithful today, and He will be faithful tomorrow.

Because God was faithful at the Red Sea, and He was faithful in the right now of the Jordan River, they could expect Him to be faithful in the next ordeal. Back in verse 13, we saw that over 40,000 men were dressed and ready for battle as they crossed into the Promised Land. They were crossing close to Jericho, which they knew was the first city they would take in the Promised Land. While they were in the middle of one scary scenario, they were already fully expecting the next! We've all had seasons when we have to deal with one struggle after another. Times when you know that you will not have a chance to rest when you get through one battle because the next one is hot on its heels. How completely exhausting!

So let's make this personal. After all, God had these accounts written down so that we would remember and use them to shape our faith and actions!

God was faithful in the Red Sea.

He is faithful right now in the Jordan River.

He will be faithful in the battle at Jericho.

6. **What is a Red Sea moment for you (something God already did)?**

7. **What is your Jordan River moment (what God is getting you through right now, or just got you through)?**

8. **If you already know what your Jericho moment will be, what is it (the next battle on your horizon)?**

9. **Repeat after me, write this down! (Copy these statements in your own handwriting!)**

God was faithful at my Red Sea.

God is faithful in the midst of my Jordan River.

God will be faithful when I face my Jericho!

That truth moves me to tears every time I think about it! Things I could never have made it through in my own power, He has brought me through! And I can trust that no matter what the circumstance, He will always come through for me! And here's the best part: He knows, far better than I do, what is best for me.

There are times when I have had the sense that God was in control of situations that turned out in ways I didn't particularly like. Later, it always turns out that what God planned (and what I would never have chosen!) was best!

10. **Can you share a time God's way was not your way but was clearly the right way?**

Say this out loud one more time before we close for the day:

God was faithful at my Red Sea.

God is faithful in the midst of my Jordan River.

God will be faithful when I face Jericho!

Week Three Small Group Note Space

Discussion Questions:

Day 1 – 1, 2, 6, 7

Day 2 – 1, 2, 5

Day 3 – 2, 3, 4, 6, 8

Day 4 – 2, 5, 10, 13

Day 5 – 4, 6, 7, 8

Use this space to record prayer requests and praises from the study group each week.

Week 4, Day 1

Preparing For a Miraculous Victory

Read Joshua 5:1-9

Verse 1 lets us know that the surrounding enemies were too scared to fight Israel, so they had a little bit of time for a much-needed pause after crossing the Jordan and before conquering Jericho. During this respite, God had Joshua round up the men for circumcision. They would surely need a few days of rest.

Circumcision was the physical mark that identified the Hebrews as God's chosen people; it was the action the people took to seal their part of the covenant. We read that all of the Hebrew men who left Egypt were circumcised, but only two of those men still lived - Joshua and Caleb. For some reason or another, circumcision was abandoned during the forty years in the desert. I haven't found a clear reason in scripture, so I wondered if it had to do with the conditions in the desert, but here they are in a temporary camp performing the minor surgeries. Whatever the human reason for neglecting circumcision for forty years, I think it pleased God to have the people physically take ownership in the covenant on the soil of the Promised Land.

Look back at verse 9. I spent a long time wondering just what the Lord meant by this statement. Then I followed a clue. It says, "So the place has been called Gilgal to this day." I looked up the translation, and found out that Gilgal means *"circle."*

1. **With that new information, what do you think was the more significant message communicated here?**

The time Israel spent in slavery in Egypt was punishment. They first were led to Egypt for a temporary rescue from famine. We know from Genesis that the famine was seven years long, and yet the people of Israel never left. They got comfortable in their temporary home and slowly found themselves in bondage. What should have been less than a decade, lasted 400 years. Then the punishment was extended through the desert years. But now, there is a new generation who have entered the land of promise! They consecrated themselves, renewed the covenant, and God brought them full circle! This moment is the time for a fresh start!

2. **When have you been given a fresh start? How did it feel?**

These first days in the Promised Land are full of beautiful connections between the people and their God. They entered by way of a visible miracle. They built a memorial, renewed the covenant through circumcision, and next they celebrated!

Read Joshua 5:10-12

To this day, people celebrate Passover by recounting the events that took place in Egypt, when God's mighty hand rescued His people! If you ever have time to learn about the Passover celebration, you'll find that it is rich in history and symbolism. For our purposes here, it is important to know that the whole community celebrated the same way. The entire family shared this meal and, throughout the meal, the conversation told the story of what happened in their final days in Egypt and their rescue. Every item of food points to something God did or something the people experienced in the original Passover.

Think about so many other holidays and days of remembrance. Some we make sure to observe no matter what (Christmas, Easter!), on some we pause and reflect for a few moments (Memorial Day, Veterans' Day), and others I don't even notice (what are you supposed to do for Arbor Day?).

3. **Which of the scheduled holidays do you celebrate whether you're feeling it or not?**

The Passover isn't just an annual obligation. It is designed to commemorate what God has done and to point to His unfailing faithfulness.

4. **What holy days do something similar for you?**

Easter and Christmas are the holy days I most look forward to every year. Thanksgiving is one I enjoy, but if I'm honest, I treat it as a dress rehearsal for Christmas. Some years I am excited about it, but in other years it is an obligation that comes up too quickly, and I am just not in the mood. But what I have come to love is that the traditions of the day force me to go through motions that get me in the right frame of mind before the day is over. At some point in the day, I can't help pausing to acknowledge just how much I have to be thankful for.

My family isn't very formal. We tend to be silly and lighthearted more often than not. So when I try to get serious on special occasions (like reading Luke 1 and 2 on Christmas Eve, or asking what everyone is thankful for during Thanksgiving dinner), I am often met with jokes or silliness at the start. I keep thinking, the older I get, the better I'll get at leading my family into reverent moments, but I'm still waiting on that to happen. Maybe we can help each other.

5. **What happens in your home on holy days that gets everyone appropriately reflective during the celebration?**

6. **Look at verse 10. Where did they celebrate the Passover?**

7. **Look back at Joshua 4:20. Where had they built the memorial?**

Gilgal is a significant place for the people of Israel, and it will come up again in our studies.

8. **One more time, what does the name Gilgal mean?**

The last thing we'll look at today is in verses 11-12.

9. **What did they finally get a taste of?**

10. **What would they never taste again?**

11. **Put yourself in their place for a moment. What do you think their reaction was the first morning there was no manna from heaven?**

12. How has God provided for you in the past, or how is He providing for you now?

13. Can you think of ways His provision has changed?

As our circumstances change and we grow, we should expect the way God provides for us to change. We can trust that He will always give us what we need when we need it, even though it is sometimes hard for us to recognize what is going on.

I began motherhood when I was 19 years old. It was hard! I was so blessed that God used my parents and in-laws to provide for us. My husband and I worked hard, but it was never enough, and we were routinely humbling ourselves to beg our parents for financial help in the early years. As time went on, we asked less often, and they volunteered help which was always welcome. I can't point back to the day or year, but at some point, that help became no longer necessary. We stopped asking and they stopped feeling the need to volunteer help in that way. It was gradual, but as our needs changed and our ability grew, our manna went away.

Imagine if the manna had continued after they had entered the land flowing with milk and honey.

14. What do you think the result would have been?

God provides for us in our need, but He is not interested in helping us to become lazy or entitled. That feels like a strong statement to make, but I am thankful for the truth in it!

15. Write out Ephesians 2:10

We are each carefully created, and God has works laid out ahead of us. We have skills to develop, passions to ignite, and abilities to share. We have stuff to do, my friends! Enjoy the respite of manna when it is there. When it is not there, enjoy what God is building in you!

Week 4, Day 2

The Fall of Jericho

Today we move from the worship-filled time of rest into some major action. And we open today's study with what was likely an unforgettable encounter for Joshua, yet the whole thing happens in three short verses!

Read Joshua 5:13-15

So much to unpack! First, who was this man with his sword drawn? Some Bible scholars say this was a *Christophany* or a pre-incarnate appearance of Jesus. Remember, Jesus is the second person of the Godhead. He exists eternally with the Father and the Holy Spirit. I tend to lean with other Bible scholars on this one, though, and think this man was more likely a warrior angel. The presence of the drawn sword is what makes me lean the way I do. Ultimately, where you fall on that detail isn't as important as recognizing that whoever this was, he represented the Lord, and had been given authority in this battle.

Next, notice that without knowing if this was friend or foe, Joshua strode right up to him and asked! Talk about bold and courageous!

1. **How did the angel answer?**

Have you ever been to a Christian sporting event? Both teams pray before the game, and somewhere in that prayer between asking for protection and fair sportsmanship is usually a request for the win! I've heard people joke that God is a fan of their team and hates the rival team. On some level, we know God doesn't choose sides!

Getting into a heavier topic, and avoiding getting political (I'm attempting to tiptoe through a minefield here!), we can look at wars the same way. While people on each side of a war tend to want God to be on their side, the reality is that He does not join human sides; we choose whether or not to be aligned with Him.

Finally, look at Joshua's response to fall on his face at the realization that the Lord had something out of the ordinary to share with him. The Commander of the Lord's Army told Joshua to remove his sandals, for they were on holy ground. The last time that happened was when the Lord spoke to Moses through a burning bush just before sending him to wage a different kind of war.

Joshua was used to hearing from God, God often gave him directives and commands for the people, but this encounter was different. And all we get to know is that the encounter happened. Was more said? I would love to know! I have a feeling God was giving Joshua the gift of knowing that he and his inexperienced army were not fighting alone.

Read 2 Kings 6:15-17

I think the encounter with the Commander of the Lord's Army gave Joshua a similar boost of confidence!

There is an awesome woman I consider an auntie in the faith who recently shared a story of her own encouraging holy encounter. While in the midst of one of life's tougher battles, she cried out to God asking Him to show her that He was with her, and she was almost immediately blessed to have a vision of Jesus walking right past her. He didn't say anything, but He didn't need to. She was given the peace she needed in the knowledge that Jesus was there.

2. **Can you think of a time when God has given you a similar gift - some unexpected sign or message to let you know that He is with you?**

Read Joshua 6:1-5 - Try to read it as if it were the first time and you have no idea how this story ends.

3. **What would you think of these instructions? Do you think you would obey?**

4. **Can you think of instances where you were ready to jump right into something, only to be told you have to go much slower than you would have liked?**

I feel like it is a running theme in my life to learn the importance of slowing down, and of going at God's pace! I am inclined to race into things the moment I have an idea, and I have learned (am learning!) that I have a much better chance at success if I slow down and take the time to plan, ask questions, seek guidance, and think through the consequences. But like the Israelites in this moment of history, sometimes there isn't anything to do with that downtime except to wait on the Lord's timing! Oh, how difficult that waiting can be!

5. **Can you think of times you rushed into something and ended up wishing you had waited?**

Read Joshua 6:6-11

6. **They were to march in silence! Has God ever told you to keep your mouth shut? And did you?**

I think that when God has told me to keep my mouth shut (which He has had to do on more occasions than I would like to admit), it has been for my benefit and the preservation of relationships. But in the case of Joshua 6, there was more to it.

7. **Why do you think the army was to march in silence?**

8. **What do you imagine was happening inside the walls of Jericho during these daily silent marches?**

Read Joshua 6:12-21

9. **List the instructions Joshua gave when it was finally time to shout and take Jericho.**

10. **Why do you think the "devoted things" were not to be taken by the army? (Look ahead to verse 24)**

11. **What sorts of things do you think the gold, silver, and bronze items were?**

It would be a good guess to say that a large number of the items were likely used in idol worship. Plenty of others were likely household objects of monetary value. Yet all of these items were off limits.

12. Why do you think all of the plunder from this first city Israel conquered was to be placed in the treasury?

It is significant that this was the first victory in the Promised Land and needed to be set apart as special. The first fruits of all that they would plunder were commanded to be set aside for God's purposes. Imagine you were going door to door collecting monetary gifts from your neighbors (just go with me!) and the first neighbor handed you $100,000 and you were commanded to give every dime of that as your tithe. Would your willingness to obey that command be influenced by whether you expected the rest of your neighbors to be as generous as the first or to answer their doors at all? I think there was an exercise in trusting God here.

As we go on in the book of Joshua, we'll see that placing their full trust in God was rewarded. Obedience was necessary. Disobedience was not tolerated.

Do Not Rebuild What The Lord Has Torn Down! Do Not Return to What God Has Rescued You From!

Read Joshua 6:22-25

Remember Rahab? I'm so glad Joshua did!

Quite a bit of time has passed since we last met Rahab. While we've been reading about what Israel has been up to, life was going on for Rahab and her family.

1. How do you imagine that time was spent?

2. **What do you think Rahab and her family were experiencing in the week the Israelite army marched around?**

3. **We tend to rush through our reading of scripture but force yourself to slow down. What must Rahab and her family have experienced on day seven?**

The silent army must have still made an immense noise with their rhythmic marching. Last week I lost my voice and had to whisper, and I was thoroughly amused that everyone responded to me in whispers when their voices were fine! It's instinct to get quiet when others are quiet. I imagine that the frightened people of Jericho got quiet during those marches. Perhaps the silence didn't last long, perhaps insults flew. But for at least a bit, I imagine total silence except for the marching. I wonder if they could feel the vibrations of the march like when I can feel the bass of my son's too-loud stereo.

And then the wall came down. This was no garden wall; it was a fortified wall surrounding the city. It was so thick that homes were built into the wall. In Joshua 2:15, we read that Rahab's home was part of the city wall. Stone walls don't come down quietly or gently.

4. **What must Rahab and her family have experienced once Joshua gave the order to yell?**

Even having been given the promise of protection, and having some inkling of faith in God, Rahab must have wondered if she would perish with the rest of the people after all. Perhaps those spies forgot her, and maybe they didn't have the authority to make a deal. What if they never made it back to their camp at all? And with the city falling around her, the terrified screams of her neighbors echoing in her ears, and the shouts of the conquering army all around, Rahab was met by those spies who remembered their promise.

Through streets filled with rubble, bodies, and soldiers killing every other survivor, Rahab and her family were led safely to the camp of Israel.

I can only imagine the emotions of fear mixed with relief that Rahab and her family were experiencing. As she left her home and headed toward safety in the form of a completely unfamiliar life, she was literally walking through a war scene. And yet she took one step after another. Probably shaky steps!

Again, we learn from Rahab! More often than we would like, we have to take one small step of faith after another by keeping our eyes focused on the promised victory ahead.

One more note on Rahab before we go on from her part in this study: look at verse 25.

5. **List who was spared because of Rahab helping the spies?**

6. **List who we know, for sure, remained among the Israelites.**

We have no idea who else if any, remained among the Israelites. But we know that because of her faith, her family had a chance to come to know God and live in relationship with Him.

7. **If you were in Rahab's place, and the family members and people "who belong to you" (for our purposes, let's translate that as the people you love and care for) in your home would be the only ones spared and given a chance at a life of faith, list who those people would be.**

Your opportunities to lead others to God may be far greater than you realize. Meditate on that for a while!

Read Joshua 6:26 and 1 Kings 16:34, which took place around 400 years later.

The curse Joshua proclaimed was most serious.

8. Why do you think this city was not to be rebuilt?

Without scripture spelling out the reason, my best guess relates to the same reason for all of the plunder of Jericho being placed into the Lord's treasury. While claiming the Promised Land was a gift to Israel, it was a punishment on the people who previously inhabited the land. They turned to other gods, and they reveled in sin. Their destruction was an example of the consequences of turning from God. It was also the oldest and most impressive fortified city. Its collapse was a warning to all others, as well as to Israel.

Now let's take a moment to be less literal and see how this applies to your life and mine today.

The directive, if I may paraphrase, is:

> **Do not rebuild what God has torn down!**
>
> **Do not return to what God has rescued you from!**

9. What has God rescued you from or torn down in your life?

As I ask this, I have to pause and ask that we get very real with each other. A frustration I hear all too often, from newer churchgoers and those who were saved in adulthood, is that they don't feel like they can talk about the real-life things they are dealing with because it would just shock everyone in the group. There are women in our churches who have been rescued from drugs, from prostitution, from addiction, from pornography, from gang life, from abuse, from compulsive lying and stealing, from ugliness that is shocking.

Some women are learning to live Christian lives while having committed unspeakable sins in their pasts. Please make your study space one where these things can be discussed safely - free from judgment and free from any chance that private testimonies and struggles would be shared with anyone else.

So I'll ask again, and if you're worried about people seeing this, you don't have to write it down, but please take time to really think about this:

10. What has God rescued you from in your life?

11. And now a very important question: Why would you ever go back?

Unfortunately, old habits die hard. If the door to sin is not completely shut, it can creep back in. When people in the church are hateful or judgmental or unwelcoming, and people from our old sinful life are nice, it is easy to confuse God's people with God and walk back to what is more comfortable. If that last sentence felt a little like a punch in the gut, I lovingly ask you to ponder your treatment of the unsaved or newly saved.

The root of any answer to "why would you go back?" is sin.

If God has rescued you from something, knocked down something in your life, **do not go back**! Resolve never to go back! Going back can only bring disaster.

I might have gotten a little strong handed there, but I think Joshua's warning in verse 26 was harsh for a reason. It needs to sink in!

Let's end on a higher note. **Read Joshua 6:27**

So the Lord was with Joshua!

Week 4, Day 4

One Man's Mistake Leads to Giant Consequences

Read Joshua 7:1

1. **Who took some of the devoted things from Jericho?**

2. **Who does it say "were unfaithful in regard to the devoted things"?**

The community was judged as a whole. It was one man who broke this command, but his community was held guilty with him. It's tempting to consider this unfair unless we grasp that God intends for believers to live with a corporate mindset, meaning that we are to live out our faith in community together. This is why we gather weekly for corporate worship. We are meant to encourage and love each other and to hold one another accountable.

Read Jesus' prayer for the Church in John 17:20-23.

Now look back at Joshua 6:18.

Achan's sin had catastrophic consequences for the entire community, just as God had warned them.

Read Joshua 7:2-3

After several miraculous victories east of the Jordan, and now coming off the heels of a huge victory at Jericho, the reputation of Joshua and Israel was spreading like wildfire, and the people of the land were terrified. Geographically, Ai was the next logical target, and they knew it. Based on the report from Joshua's scouts, what should the battle at Ai look like?

Read Joshua 7:4-5

Ai should have been an easy target, but Israel was defeated badly. Embarrassingly, even.

3. **Look at how their resulting fear is described. What is significant about this?**

Read Joshua 7:6-9

The act of tearing their clothes and sprinkling dust over their heads was a display of mourning. Joshua mourned the men who were killed. More than that, though, I think Joshua mourned the loss of God's favor. He was well aware that their victory came only at the hand of God, so this defeat meant that God had chosen not to help.

Reading between the lines, I think Joshua was completely unaware of Achan's sin at Jericho. I believe he was so awed at God's might that he didn't think for a moment that anyone else would disregard God's orders. So for Joshua, and probably for the elders who mourned at his side, the defeat at Ai made no sense.

4. **When Joshua prayed, what did his words reveal about what he was thinking?**

We looked at a similar situation back in Joshua 2 when the spies' plan seemed to go off course. When things go wrong, it is natural to start questioning. It is normal to get a bit irrational, knowing all that Joshua knew about God's plans for Israel, it was definitely irrational to think they should have been content to remain next to the Promised Land instead of in it.

5. **Have you ever felt like God was leading you to something, and when you were close to it, decided that was good enough?**

Picture this with me. You desperately need $100, and a friend says they want to gift you $100. This friend has an unlimited cash flow, and you know it will please this friend to be generous to you. In fact, you know this friend is so generous, she is likely to give you more than you need. She begins to count out the cash and places the bills in your hand as she goes. When she gets to $95, would you say, "Oh, that's good enough."? Of course not!

God's resources are limitless. His ability is limitless. His goodness, generosity, and power are limitless, and we should want the fullness of His promises! We should be content with what He has planned for us, but we should never be content to settle for less than what God wants for us!

While the grief caused Joshua to question everything, he did the exact right thing with his questions: he took them to God. God welcomes such an honest conversation with us.

Read God's response in Joshua 7:10-15

6. **Write out God's words from verse 10!**

I love that God is so patient and so direct with Joshua! He makes the reason for their circumstance clear, and tells Joshua what to do about it, and even goes so far as to help in the process of making things right. Again, people are to consecrate themselves.

This chapter only names Achan as one who kept devoted things. I wonder - and these are only my own thoughts - whether other people had also taken devoted things. If they had, then after the defeat at Ai when they were told to consecrate themselves, what action would they have to take to dedicate themselves for the Lord? Is it possible that others had committed the same sin, but repented by getting rid of those devoted items when told to consecrate themselves? I don't know whether it happened that way or not. All we know for sure is that Achan did not use the time of consecration that way.

Read Joshua 7:16-23

I can think of so many times when my children have been busted for something, but they clung to a story of innocence. It used to frustrate me to no end. How long would it take for them to realize I'm not fooled? One such moment stands out to me. My son was in kindergarten and he, as so many children do, pondered the effects of scissors. Do they only cut paper? What would happen if they made contact with one's hair? And with the wisdom of a kindergartner, the most logical place to test out the effectiveness of scissors on hair would be the hair he could see the best, right in the middle of his forehead! And all the way down to the scalp!

As a hairdresser by trade, I have to think the look of horror on my face was more extreme than that of the average mother in the same situation, but maybe we would all experience maximum horror at that moment. Either way, my reaction was pretty extreme, and probably made the poor kid think his best course of action was to convince me that the hair simply fell off! There was no question in my mind as to his guilt, but he clung to his lie fiercely.

That was a learning experience for both of us, and I can look back at the moment now with a sense of humor. But Achan was a grown man. The consequences of his deceit were much more severe. His clinging to an appearance of innocence is not cute, and would not become an amusing anecdote.

Read Joshua 7:24-26

I don't enjoy these verses. They aren't "feel good." And yet, they are necessary. Achan knew what had been commanded, and he chose to disobey.

I had a professor once who said that the good news doesn't mean much unless you first know the bad news. Meaning the good news that Christ's death and resurrection give you the invitation to eternal life in His presence means more when you recognize that the alternative is that we all have sinned and deserve death and eternal separation from God.

The people of Israel had witnessed the extreme consequences of God's favor, and at the Valley of Achor, they witnessed the extreme consequence of disobedience and the loss of God's favor. They also had to be the ones to carry out justice as a community to restore order.

7. **Why do you think they had to carry out the punishment themselves?**

Let's close today's study on a high note. **Read Joshua 8:1-2**

Restoration had occurred.

Week 4, Day 5

Victory at Ai and a Renewed Covenant

Today the mood picks back up!

Read Joshua 8:1-8

1. **How were God's directives different (from Jericho) in this battle?**

2. **What do you think Achan would have thought if he had known about this change - that Jericho's plunder was to be a tithe, and all of the rest would be for the people to keep?**

We don't always know what is coming next. Our obedience can't be dependent on knowing the whole story. We must trust in God's character; His will is always best, and He wants good things for us. His commands are always in our best interest. Our obedience has to be decided when we have no idea what comes next.

I find it interesting that it was on their second advance on Ai that God revealed to the people that the rules would be different now that they were past the first city.

3. **Come to think of it, what direction did they have from God the first time they went after Ai?**

Is it possible that there was no direction before that first attack on Ai because they didn't ask for any? Have you ever found yourself trying to make sense of something only to realize you forgot to talk to God before making a decision or taking action?

4. **How many men went against Ai in the first battle? (Joshua 7:4)**

5. **This time, all of the fighting men were a part of the battle. What do you take away from this difference?**

6. **Why do you think Joshua placed himself in the group that would look like cowards running away from Ai's forces?**

Read Joshua 8:9-22

To really comprehend how this battle went down, in the box below, mark where Israel's forces were strategically stationed. As I was reading, I got hung up on the numbers not making much sense to me, so I did some research. It turns out the word translated as "thousand" in Joshua 8:3 has dual meaning and is the same word that is translated as "Chiefs" in Genesis 36:15. Because this group was hiding, and they were directed to stay close to the city (v.4), the smaller number makes sense to me, but let's focus more on their position than their number. Let's look at the details we have to work with; Joshua 8:11 describes the front of the city as facing north. That would suggest those hiding behind the city were situated at the south - either 30 Chiefs, or 30,000 men. Verse 12 places 5,000 men between Bethel and Ai, to the west of the city.

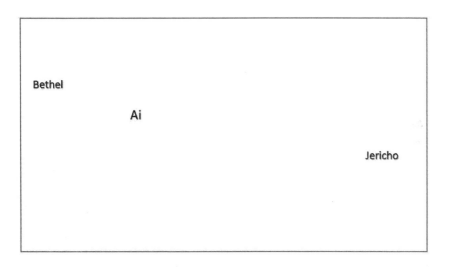

This strategy God provided Joshua was brilliantly effective. The people of Ai never saw it coming and were perhaps all the more unconcerned after having beaten the Israelites so badly the first time.

7.   **What are your thoughts after seeing God's battle plan play out?**

Read Joshua 8:23-29

Some gory details, I know. This is a book that chronicles a lot of war, and war is a bloody business. Rather than focusing on the ick factor, look at the total obedience Joshua and Israel displayed. Joshua held out his javelin toward Ai through almost the entire battle. I've never held a javelin myself, but can you imagine the muscle fatigue?

8. **Comparing the battle of Jericho with this second battle at Ai, what is the most obvious difference in the battle strategy?**

I always thought it was funny that the battle at Jericho didn't involve any real fighting by human hands. The closest thing to battle for them was slaying the survivors after God caused the wall to crumble. This time, God provided the battle plan, but the fighting was all done by the people. Lives were lost, and many more would be lost. I think it was important that the people felt the weight of that. Even in war, the taking of lives cannot be taken lightly.

Israel has been on an emotional roller coaster! There was the high of crossing the Jordan, the reflective time of consecration, the celebration of the Passover, the high of victory at Jericho followed by an extreme low with the sin of Achan and the defeat at Ai, and finally, reconciliation with God led to an incredible and total Victory at Ai. It was time to worship the Lord!

Read Joshua 8:30-35

Mount Ebal and Mount Gerizim are approximately 30 miles north of Ai, so as the people traveled there, they had some time to reflect on all that they had witnessed.

9. **What do you think would be running through your mind on that journey?**

10. **List what actions were taken at Mount Ebal and Mount Gerizim.**

1.

2.

3.

4.

Read Deuteronomy 27:1-8

Logistically, Israel had to battle Jericho and Ai before they could carry out this action.

11. What would have happened if they had tried to go right to these mountains after crossing the Jordan?

Spiritually, I think it was also necessary for the people to go through all that they had before their trip to the mountain.

12. How do you think their experiences so far impacted their time of worship and renewal of the covenant at Mount Ebal and Mount Gerizim?

13. Can you relate? When have trials deepened your understanding of who God is and how He loves you?

Reflecting on such occasions often brings tears, but I promise it is not my goal to dredge up difficult times with no purpose! I shared before that I was very private about what I didn't understand early in my walk with God and that because of that, I didn't receive much guidance. I had to go through many trials and rescues before I learned to recognize how God used those to bring me closer to Him, to grow my trust in Him, and to teach me.

While I don't want to cause you sadness in remembering your trials, I do want to encourage you to *share* the joy of your rescues and all that God did for you through those situations with others who are in the middle of their own battles, or whose battles have yet to begin. Show them what hope looks like.

A good student of the Bible could list off many, many things that are true about God and His character, but that is merely academic. There are things we know about God because we have read them, and if we believe that the Bible is the true word of God, then we even believe those things. But there are other things we know to be true of God because we have the first-hand experience.

Close today's study by listing the things you know from first-hand experience to be true of God, and then spend some time in worship, thanking Him for these revelations.

Week Four Small Group Note Space

Discussion Questions:

Day 1 – 4, 5, 11, 13

Day 2 – 2, 4, 5, 7

Day 3 – 1, 7, 9, 11

Day 4 – 4, 7

Day 5 – 3, 7, 12, 13

Use this space to record prayer requests and praises from the study group each week.

Tricked Into a Treaty & The Southern Campaign

Read Joshua 9:1-6

1. What measures did the Gibeonites take to trick Israel into making a peace treaty with them?

2. Where had the Israelites set up camp again?

Note the location of Gibeon on the map near the end of today's lesson.

Read Joshua 9:7-15

To their credit, Israel remembered that they were not to make any peace treaties with the people in Canaan, and they asked the right questions of the delegation. They had good intentions. But verse 14 makes their mistake clear.

3.   What did the Israelites fail to do?

I can identify with this mistake because I have made it countless times. There have been so many instances where it never even occurred to me to pray before making a decision or taking some action. It tends to be my habit to think through things logically, and if the next step is unclear or I cannot decide, then I'm likely to seek out advice, usually even godly counsel, and if I'm still unclear, I would likely end up at prayer. Remember, this is my default habit, not my advice! My advice would be to make prayer your first step, place prayer in between every other step, and pray after you have done everything else!

4.   Why do you suppose we tend to place prayer so far down the list of actions or leave it off the list entirely?

Read Joshua 9:16-27

5.   Why did the Israelites keep their end of the treaty?

6.   What did the leaders of Israel do to make things as right as possible?

Read Joshua 10:1-4

7.   What do we learn about the city of Gibeon?

Read Joshua 10:5

Note the locations of each of these tribal groups on the map in the back of this book. This collection of fighters was a large army that had assembled against Gibeon!

Read Joshua 10:6-10

Once again, the Lord said to Joshua, "Do not be afraid," and He assured Joshua that Israel would have victory. We also read that Israel took the enemy by surprise.

8.   Why do you think they were surprised when Israel showed up to defend Gibeon?

I think in human terms, it would be unexpected for Israel to defend Gibeon - it was already shocking that they honored the treaty in letting Gibeon live, but to protect them was completely unexpected. Add in the fact that the Israelites marched all night from Gilgal (look back at the map for reference); this suggests some serious determination on the part of Israel. It brings to mind Jesus' instruction to turn the other cheek. The way we are called to love people is radical and unexpected but, as God's people, we should be shockingly different! We should be so different that people who watch us wonder what could be the cause!

Read Joshua 10:11-15

The sun and moon did what, now? This whole scene amazes me! At Jericho, God did the fighting. At Ai, God provided the plan but had the people do all of the fighting. But now, look at verse 11. God joined the people in this one!

9.   Why do you think God chose to fight alongside his people this time?

Let's focus on that hail. The Israelites were right in the mix swinging their swords, protected while God's perfect aim only took out the enemy.

Now, let's look at the extended day. Wow! What would you do with 12 extra hours in a day?

I could definitely use more hours most days, but my uses for them would be nowhere near as important as what was happening in Joshua 10! After marching all night, and fighting for several hours, Joshua asked for more time so that they could complete the victory.

10. Why would he ask for that, instead of getting a good night's sleep and resuming the battle the next day?

Read Joshua 10:16-27

I find it almost humorous that Joshua's order was to lock the kings up in their hiding place while they finished off their defeat of the armies. But then when they come back to deal with the kings, there is nothing funny about it. Look at verse 25; in the middle of this very serious moment, Joshua pauses to preach to his people. "Be strong and courageous. This is what the Lord will do to the enemies you are going to fight."

Joshua 10:28-43 summarizes the battles which followed. Note the locations of the conquered cities and areas on the map from earlier in this lesson:

Makkedah, Libnah, Lachish, Gezer, Eglon, Hebron, Debir. The Negev (or Negeb), the western foothills, from Kadesh Barnea to Gaza, from the region of Goshen to Gibeon.

If you look at the whole of Israel and color in all of the places they have conquered, Israel took nearly the entire south of the Promised Land. The only region in the south not yet conquered at this point is the land of the Philistines.

This series of battles came about as a result of a mistake Joshua and the leaders made by entering into a treaty with Gibeon without seeking the Lord. Yet look at the awe-inducing victory God delivered!

11. Why do you think this mistake was followed up with such victory instead of punishment?

My thoughts? God looks at the heart. He knew their intentions were pure, and He saw that they were learning. This mistake was part of their learning process; there was no intent to deceive or circumvent God's commands. One of the truths I know about God from personal experience is that He can bring beauty out of ashes. He can bring good things out of our mistakes.

When looking at the battles that Israel fought in the Promised Land, strategists divide them into military campaigns. The Central Campaign won Jericho, Ai, and Gibeon for Israel. These were large and influential cities. The Southern Campaign is what we have studied today. We don't know just how long all of those battles took, or how much time had passed before Gibeon tricked Israel, or between that time and Gibeon needing help. But the pace of Joshua makes it feel like all of this is happening very quickly.

Chapter 10 ends with Israel returning to camp at Gilgal. Gilgal should be getting familiar by now; this is the place Israel camped when they first entered the Promised Land, and it has served as home base for Israel so far.

Week 5, Day 2

The Northern Campaign

Read Joshua 11:1-5 and note the locations of the cities and areas on the map at the back of this book, as many as you are able. There is no shame in using a magnifying glass!

This army is the largest Israel has faced so far. They were also the most formidable with horses and chariots and sheer numbers. Can you guess what God will say to Joshua?

Read Joshua 11:6

Do not be afraid! I did not expect what came next, however. This battle would put Israel up against the largest army they have faced yet.

1. **How long did God say it would last?**

When I think of my greatest battles, I don't think any have been won in under 24 hours. But it seems like God usually brings victories in ways I would never foresee. His view is of the whole picture - not just every aspect of a situation at the moment, but the ripples and ripples of consequences and results of actions and decisions, and everything before and after. His timing and solutions are perfect. I also think He takes pleasure in being unpredictable. And often He brings solutions in ways that can only point the glory to Himself! Aren't you so grateful that He makes Himself known so that in the next trial there is no question as to whom we should turn?

2. **Do you have a testimony of God bringing about victory in a way that could only be God?**

Now can we have a moment of silence for those poor horses? It's things like this that made me wonder whether I was hearing God correctly when He led *me,* a girl who loves animals and closes her eyes at violent movie scenes, to a study out of the book of Joshua! In case you are not familiar, to hamstring a horse means to cut its hamstring, which renders it lame. It could not recover from such an injury, and even if it were to survive, it would be no good for work or breeding, and so those horses were left to die a slow and painful death.

Horses and chariots made an army exponentially more efficient, and for an army lacking horses and chariots to go against them would be suicide. This strategy (to hamstring the horses and burn the chariots) that God gave Joshua was militarily brilliant. I learned that part of what made this such an effective military move, beyond taking away the enemy's advantage, is that the sound the horses made was so loud and troubling that they threw the army into panic and confusion.

That detail just made this scene even more troubling to me. I have talked this through with anyone who would humor me, and I keep saying, I just want one more verse to tell me God had them go back after the fighting and put the horses out of their misery, or that the horses died quickly. I have tried and tried, for your sake as well as my own, to find some pretty way to look at this, something to give it a happily ever after, and it just doesn't exist. Here's what I finally feel God teaching me through this struggle I've had: War, however necessary, is always ugly and the cost is high and tragic. For victory to occur, those horses had to be the sacrifice; that's all there was to it.

And how can we not draw the connection to Jesus Christ? Like war, our sin is always ugly, and the cost is high and tragic. For us to have victory, Christ had to sacrifice Himself to atone for our sin and rise again, conquering death, so that we can have eternal life. Joshua and his people were about to claim the glorious Promised Land, and the inheritance we are preparing to take hold of is infinitely better.

I joked about a moment of silence for the horses, but do take a quiet moment now, reflect on the genuine sacrifice that was made for you, and express your gratitude to Jesus.

Read Joshua 11:7-15

3. **Joshua burned Jericho, Ai, and now Hazor. What did these cities have in common?**

4. **Why would they not have destroyed the rest of the cities (v. 13)?**

After the fighting was over, the people of Israel would finally settle in the land. Once the buildings were empty, they would be perfectly adequate for living. After fighting for so long, it would be nice to have move-in ready homes!

There were many cities to be conquered once their kings and armies had lost at the Waters of Merom. We don't have much detail about this campaign at all past the miraculous one-day victory.

5. **Why do you think there wasn't more detail about this final campaign?**

Read Joshua 11:16-23

This passage summarizes all three campaigns. It was not 100% of the Promised Land; there was still much to be done, but this was a vast majority, and enough that they could finally have a bit of a break.

Let's spend a moment on verse 20. Many people struggle with the idea that God would harden someone's heart, their logic being that this is contrary to God's gift of free will to humankind. I had to wrestle with this myself.

Read Genesis 15:13-16, especially verse 16.

The people in the land, whose hearts were hardened in Joshua 11:20, had been given time in which they could have turned to God. They had 400 years while Israel was enslaved in Egypt, plus a bonus 40 years while they camped in the wilderness. A word study yields something interesting. The word translated as "harden" is *"chazaq"* in Hebrew. It has many meanings including *to seize, be strong, confirm, be sure,* etc. It is the same word used the many times Joshua was told to be strong and courageous, and when Moses was told to encourage Joshua. It is clear that God did not cause the people to choose a negative path; He confirmed what was in their hearts, and their time was up.

It is a harsh reality for all of us; that time will eventually be up.

6. **Does this understanding of the phrase "harden their hearts" make you think differently?**

The last sentence in this chapter states, "Then the land had rest from war." Not the people, but the land, the ground.

7. **What do you think is the significance to the land having rest from war?**

There's a whole science to giving fields a season of rest, and God commanded such seasons of rest in farming. You can feel free to Google for real details, but the bottom line is that the earth needs a season of rest to replenish nutrients so that it can continue to be useful.

Many Scriptures refer to God as the God of all the earth. I think we sometimes forget that He created all the earth, not just us. He takes care of and has concern for more than only humans.

8. What else could use a season of rest to remain useful?

I'd love to know what you wrote down, but I sure hope you put yourself on that list! We need rest, and God designed the Sabbath for just that reason! Yes, the earth in Canaan/Israel had a time of rest from war, but so did the people. They needed to establish a new normal. They needed to learn to cultivate this new land and enjoy it for a bit.

9. Close today by committing to some time you will set aside for yourself to rest in the next few days.

Week 5, Day 3

Settling

We have made it through 11 chapters in Joshua! There is a shift in the writing now. We have been reading what felt like a story, but now Joshua has to cover some business. Chapter 12 summarizes all of the lands that were won under Moses' leadership east of the Jordan River, and all that was won under Joshua's leadership west of the Jordan River.

Read Joshua 13:1-7

Several years have passed since the land was given rest from war. Keep in mind that Joshua was the most likely author of the majority of this book.

1. **How does Joshua describe himself in 13:1?**

2. **How does God describe Joshua in 13:1?**

There is no deep, theological reason for me to point that out, I just think it's funny! It does make me wonder, though, just how much time had passed, and whether God was simply alerting Joshua that it was time to take the next steps, or if the people had grown comfortable and were in danger of settling for "good enough" and needed to a push.

It was a habit of the Israelites to get comfortable with their situations until the situation was really bad; that's how they ended up in slavery in Egypt for 400 years. And they are not alone in that tendency. It is uncomfortable to rock the boat sometimes!

When my daughter was a baby, she had colic, and it was an awful thing to try and get her to sleep. So often I had things to do, like chase my three-year-old around, but if the baby was able to fall asleep while laying on my chest (about the only way she did sleep for months!), I didn't dare move her. The uncomfortable position was easier to deal with than the possibility of waking her and having her little belly cause her to wail. Recently there has been a viral video circulating, in which a mom is lying next to a crib, and once the child falls asleep she commando crawls out of the room very slowly and awkwardly. I laughed hard enough to cry because that mom could have been me! I did that more than once!

3. **Have you ever stayed in a job you hated because leaving that job might be worse? Or remained in any other situation that wasn't the greatest because it also wasn't the worst?**

We just read that there was still a great deal of land to be conquered, and many enemies to drive out of the land. The next several chapters detail the boundaries of the land allotted to each tribe. We will not follow this part verse by verse in this study. However, I do encourage you to read it, and I will provide a map to help it all make sense. It goes through Chapter 21.

4. **It might be tempting to call those chapters boring, but what would be the purpose of writing down exactly what land belonged to which people in such detail?**

Remember Caleb? Caleb was one of the 12 spies Moses sent to investigate the Promised Land, and he was the one who spoke up when ten of the spies insisted that the inhabitants of the land were too big and scary! After the study we've been doing, isn't that all the more absurd? What courage that must have taken for Caleb! In week one, we talked about how frustrating it must have been for Caleb to wait through forty years in the desert for the disobedience and lack of faith of the others. Now it's Caleb's moment!

Read Joshua 14:6-15

What must it have felt like, after so many years, to finally be given his choice of land on which to settle his family? Forty-five years prior, he had spied out all of the Promised Land, or at least a lot of it, and he saw a particular plot of land that seemed perfect to him. And because of His faithfulness and patience, his heart's desire was now his.

As you do read through chapters 14-21, see if you can locate the borders and landmarks described in the Scripture using the map at the back of this book.

Week 5, Day 4

He Wants Good Things For You

We closed our last lesson by looking at chapters 14-21 of Joshua, as the inheritance of each tribe was listed out. Now we need to look a little more closely at some of the details provided in that long list of boundaries. Today we will pull out some interesting details from those chapters.

Read Joshua 15:14-19

This story is one that I would love to have more information about! Why does scripture include this incident? Charles H. Spurgeon gave a sermon on this pericope (a chunk of scripture) and looked at it as a parable on prayer. That doesn't mean it wasn't a real incident, but he drew a beautiful parallel. Aksah (the daughter; your Bible may have her name spelled differently) urged her husband to ask her father for more than what they received. The implication is that he was unwilling to ask, though we don't know why. Spurgeon suggests he was reluctant to seem ungrateful since he had already received a wife and choice land. Aksah, on the other hand, was a child of one who she knew to be generous and full of love for her, and so she was confident that she could present her request to him and expect a positive result.

I recently heard a story of a woman on her death bed who welcomed a visitor's offer to pray for her because she could not pray herself. She reasoned that she had done so much wrong that God wouldn't listen to her. This woman is not alone. Too many people in this world are unaware that the Father loves them in spite of all the wrong. The Father longs to hear from them! The Father wants a restored relationship!

There are also many believers who are quick to ask the Lord for the obvious, big things, or who find it easier to make requests for other people. But they hesitate to ask for *everything* they need or desire because "it isn't important enough," or, "He has so many bigger things to worry about," as if God's attention and ability were as limited as our own. That is not the case! God wants to hear from us. He wants us to invite Him into even the most mundane parts of our lives so that we are fully living in communion with Him!

1.   **For what have you hesitated to ask the good Lord? Ask now! The answer will either be "Yes," "Not yet," or, "I have something better in mind for you!"**

Read Joshua 17:14-18

2.   **What was the complaint?**

3.   **Summarize Joshua's response.**

4.   **Looking at how Joshua responded, do you think he had learned from Moses' frustration in leading a nation of complainers? What do you think of his handling of the situation?**

5. Now we're going to dig into a few verses that shed some light on what the nation of Israel will be dealing with for centuries. **Look at each of the verses below and note what we learn.**

Joshua 15:63

Joshua 16:10

Joshua 17:12-13

Judges 1:30

Judges 1:31

Judges 1:33

The Israelites failed to drive out **all** of the inhabitants of the land entirely.

6. **Why do you think God wanted them to drive out the inhabitants of the land entirely?**

Read Judges 10:6

7. **What did the people do which angered God?**

Read 2 Samuel 5:6

8. **What people group was David forced to deal with many generations later?**

For any of the idol-worshiping inhabitants to remain in the land, their idols and evil ways stayed with them. The remaining inhabitants would naturally feel a claim to the land and would forever be at odds with the Israelites. Their presence would naturally lead to conflict and war. The presence of false idols would be a constant temptation.

The Old Testament is full of accounts of the conflicts with the remaining inhabitants, and Israel's inability to remain faithful to the Lord. Thankfully, it is also a testament to God's unwavering love for His people, and His infinite grace and ability to forgive and rescue!

9. **Hop online and take a glance at a modern map of the very land we've been studying and compare it to the maps we looked at last week. What do you notice?**

By failing to be fully obedient to God's instructions, the people brought thousands of years of trouble down upon themselves.

Before we accidentally get too hard on the Israelites of Joshua's day, let's reflect on the fact that they are only the example we are studying. Their failure is a reflection of our own. We, humankind, are quick to let ourselves off the hook for total obedience. We get busy, distracted, or we don't want to keep working, and we fail over and over. The picture the Old Testament paints shows us that since the fall, we are incapable of a sinless life. Humankind was in desperate need of the Savior we meet in the New Testament! Thank God for His grace!

10. Is this bringing to mind any areas in which you need to fully obey God, where you may have been holding back?

11. Take some time in prayer to allow God to reveal to you any areas where you may need to reevaluate your obedience.

That got heavy, I know, but we have to take all of what Scripture has for us to learn! Now, let's move on and look at the inheritance given to the Levites.

12. Why were the Levites different from everyone else? (Hint: Joshua 18:7)

Read Exodus 32:25-29

13. How would you describe the Levites?

The Levites were the tribe descended from Jacob's son, Levi. While Moses was up on the mountain, so many fellow Israelites were worshiping a golden calf. Because of the Levites' faithfulness to God and their service in the aftermath, they were designated as servants of the Lord. The Levites were not the only ones who refrained from worshiping the false idol, but they were the ones who boldly stood against that sin.

Since the Levites were set apart from the other tribes as servants of the Lord, they would not receive a portion of land in the same way the other tribes would. Still, they had the basic human needs of a place to live and food to eat. The offerings of the whole nation of Israel would, in part, support the Levites. As for places to live, they scattered throughout the entire land of Israel and were given land within the inheritances of the other tribes. Joshua 21 details the towns assigned to the Levites.

14. What does Joshua 21:42 say each of these towns provided for the Levites?

Last week we saw that Caleb's faithfulness was remembered and rewarded.

15. What was Caleb's reward?

Read Joshua 19:49-50

16. What was Joshua's reward?

During their time in the desert, it was the Levites, Caleb, and Joshua who were faithful to the Lord without exception. Each was vocal and conspicuous in their faithfulness to God when it was the farthest thing from popular. They stood up for righteousness and obedience when no one around them did.

17. Can you think of examples like this today?

18. I long to be counted in that group. I know I have a long way to go. **With 10 being perfect boldness, and 1 being completely cowardly, where would you rank your boldness in standing up for God?**

19. What command has been repeated more than any other in this book we've been studying?

It is my prayer that we would take that command to heart and get better and better at being strong and courageous! I want to be bold and fearless in every aspect of life, but especially when it comes to sharing the gospel of Christ and standing up for faithfulness.

Wherever you ranked yourself, do not let your less-than-a-10 be a source of shame, but rather, let it inform your prayer life. This is one of those times our Father longs to hear from us and desires to grow us! Ask Him to move you closer to 10 on that scale, and He will do it! That's a promise; seize it!

Week 5, Day 5

Prayer

Yesterday we read about Caleb's daughter, Aksah. She knew she could expect her father to give her what she needed and desired, and she had no qualms about approaching him with her request.

Read Matthew 7:9-12, where Jesus expands on this truth of a parent's love.

1. What is the lesson Jesus wants us to understand?

The importance of consulting God through prayer has come up enough times through the book of Joshua that it is worth pausing to focus on for a bit. Because I want this study to be valuable to you no matter where you are in your knowledge of the Bible and all things religious, and because far too many believers look at prayer as a wish list, we're going to cover this topic at it's most basic level.

Simply put, prayer is a conversation between you and God.

Throughout Scripture, God describes Himself as your parent and your friend, as well as your Creator and the Almighty One. That's how He wants to have conversations with you. We need to approach Him with reverence, because of who He is, but He also invites us to be familiar. We can talk to Him honestly. He already knows what you think and how you feel, so there is no need to pretend politeness. We can talk to Him about anything. No topic is off limits. Nothing is too insignificant or too much for Him to handle. We can speak to Him with confidence.

Assuming particular postures (closing your eyes, bowing your head, removing a hat, falling on your knees, whatever you may do) can help you to focus, and may help to tune out everything else. Such postures are not necessary, though. If you're driving when you choose to pray, the rest of us would love for you to keep your eyes open! Prayers do not need to be formal; they do not need to include any particular words or fancy language.

When we talk to God, we can ask Him for whatever burdens us (needs and desires of our own or for others), but we also need to spend time thanking Him for what He has already done. We also need to spend some of that time in worship, adoring Him for who He is. We - the whole body of believers - are called His bride. I've learned in my marriage that telling my husband what I love about him does two things: 1) to hear how I see him builds him up, and 2) it reminds me just how great he is. The reverse is true as well, of course.

A few years ago one of my cousins who had been a friend to me was on life support, so my mother and I flew out to give his mother some help and a chance to rest. By the time we got there, my cousin was being given only palliative care, meaning they were controlling his pain, but nothing more could be done to improve his condition; they were preparing us for the end of life. It was an emotional time for all of us, and one afternoon I made my way to the hospital's chapel. At that moment I had no idea how to pray, and I found myself simply stating what I knew to be true of God.

God, You are good. You love me. You love him. You are Sovereign. You are holy. You are merciful. You are mighty. You are the healer. You are stronger than anything. You are more powerful than anything. You are...

I prayed like that for at least an hour. When I was too emotionally spent to keep going, I just sat there in the quiet, overwhelmed by the peace that flooded over me. I sensed God's presence in a nearly tangible way and didn't want the moment to end. The circumstance I was in the middle of was tragic, and yet everything I know to be true of God in the good times was true then. That is a peace that surpasses understanding.

Prayer is for us to talk to God, but it is also for us to listen to Him. In that chapel, the time I spent in silence was possibly more valuable than the time I spent speaking. Setting aside time just to be quiet, ready to receive something from God is often overlooked.

Read Habakkuk 2:1

This passage is set in a time when Israel was in turmoil. Most of the people had turned away from the Lord, many had been taken captive, more enemies had their eyes set on the rest, and the few faithful were crying out for God to do something. They sent Habakkuk to speak to God for them. The verse you just read comes right after he voiced their complaints to God.

2.   What was he going to do until he got an answer?

I want to close today's study with a little scavenger hunt of sorts. The book of Psalms is filled with prayer after prayer, and there are dozens more scattered through Scripture. Mary's song (Luke 1:46-55) is one of my favorites. Look through some of those, find one or two that speak to your heart, and either write them out or list where you saw them. There is no shame in doing an Internet search to lead you to what you're looking for, but do go back to your own Bible once you've searched. A helpful search might be, "Prayers in the Bible about _____."

Week Five Small Group Note Space

Discussion Questions:

Day 1 – 10, 11

Day 2 – 2, 6

Day 3 – 3, 4

Day 4 – 4, 6, 10, 17, 19

Day 5 – 2

Use this space to record prayer requests and praises from the study group each week.

Week 6, Day 1

Refuge

Today we get to look at a beautiful, merciful part of the nation designed by God! He thinks of everything!

Read Exodus 21:13-14

1. **How were intentional and accidental murders to be handled?**

Read Joshua 20:1-3

2. **Who were the Cities of Refuge designated to protect?**

3.   What does this tell you about God?

Read Joshua 20:4-6

4.   How were those who accidentally committed murder protected?

5.   What were they guaranteed once they presented themselves at a City of Refuge?

6.   If found innocent, they were sent back to live in the City of Refuge for how long?

7.   Why would the death of the presiding High Priest be the impetus for those sentenced to live in the City of Refuge after being found guilty of murder, yet innocent of malice aforethought?

Blood was required to atone for sin, both intentional and unintentional. The magnitude of all of our sin was the reason Jesus the Christ was the only perfect sacrifice capable of atoning for all of our sins. Hebrews 7 describes Jesus as our High Priest.

Read Hebrews 7:18-28

It is possible that the death of the High Priest was designated so that people would not necessarily be serving a life sentence in the Cities of Refuge. These cities preserved their life, but also caused them to be separated from their families. There is also significance in their death serving as the blood sacrifice which atoned for the accidental sin that had been committed and led to the temporary (but potentially years or decades long) banishment.

Read Deuteronomy 19

8. How many Cities of Refuge were they instructed to have?

9. What was significant in the locations of the Cities of Refuge?

10. Did this provision of refuge protect malicious murderers?

11. What was required to convict a person of a crime?

12. What was God's reason for providing Cities of Refuge?

Read Joshua 20:7-9

13. Which Cities became Cities of Refuge?

14. **Why would they have more cities designated in Joshua 20 than initially required in Deuteronomy 19:2? (Hint: Deuteronomy 19:9)**

I think it is incredible that our God loves us enough to offer protection when we make mistakes. And unfathomable that He would not only provide but be the atoning sacrifice for our sins. His character is unchanging. His grace is limitless. I don't want to hog all of the reflective awe here!

15. **As you consider what we have just studied, what are your thoughts?**

16. **Look up the following verses, and write what they tell you about God as your refuge.**

Psalm 7:1-5

Psalm 11

Psalm 46

Isaiah 25

Today's study has required a lot of work from you and, if you stuck with it, you undoubtedly gained some rewarding insights from that work! The verses we just looked at show that when God's people see just how merciful God is and how strongly He protects us by His own choice, we should be deeply moved! So try something today; whether you share it is entirely up to you, but please give it a go.

17. **To close today's study, write out your own psalm, recognizing God as your refuge. Your psalm does not need to be fancy poetry or use language from Biblical times. It should just be your reverence for God poured out in your own style. Consider this an act of worship.**

Week 6, Day 2

Jumping To Conclusions

When we enter today's lesson, we find Joshua and the rest of the Israelites in Shiloh. Since the time the land was given rest from war, Shiloh has served as the central camp for Israel. Throughout chapters 14 - 21, Joshua has been ruling from Shiloh. Use the map in the back of this book as you go through today's lesson.

Read Joshua 22:1-9

This moment was what these two and a half tribes had worked for and waited on for years! They had left behind their families so they could fulfill their promise to help the rest of Israel claim the Promised Land. They have endured years of fighting and conquering, and now - finally - the job is done, and they can head home.

They had been at Shiloh with the rest of the Hebrews. The Tent of Meeting had been set up there, as the people had gathered at Shiloh before taking up their inheritances and settling in their assigned lands. While they were probably relieved and even elated to be going to their own homes, they were possibly hesitant to leave the proximity of the Tabernacle.

Read Joshua 22:10

The two and a half tribes built an imposing altar in Geliloth, which is more often called Gilgal.

1.   **Why do you think they chose that location for this altar? (Look back at Joshua 4:19-22)**

Back when God stopped the flow of the Jordan River to allow the multitude of Israel into the Promised Land, they set up camp in Gilgal and built a memorial from 12 stones they carried out from the middle of the dry river bed. That was to be a reminder for generations to come of what the Lord had done.

2.   **What did we learn the name Gilgal means?**

Now, this is where my imagination takes over because Scripture doesn't give us the details, but I imagine there were some high emotions among the men heading home to claim their inheritance and reunite with family. I think that when they came to Gilgal, memories flooded back and they were astounded at all the Lord had done. I wonder if they might have a twinge of regret for settling on the far side of the Jordan. I picture them coming to the 12 stones and feeling the weight of the moment.

My thoughts? I think they knew this location was already one that all of Israel would refer to in remembrance of all that God had done. It held significance already, so their addition would not be overlooked.

Read Joshua 22: 11-20

3.   **What did the rest of Israel think was going on at Gilgal?**

4. Placing yourself in their shoes, can you see what they were afraid of?

Read Joshua 22: 21-29

5. What did the two and a half tribes say their motivation was?

6. Placing yourself in their shoes, did they have a good reason for building this altar?

Read Joshua 22:30-34

I can't help feeling like there was a dramatic overreaction here on the part of the western tribes toward the eastern two and a half tribes. The overreaction reveals that there is at least a little bit of "Us vs. Them" mentality. To be fair, the two and a half tribes were the ones who decided to claim land east of the Jordan - God allowed them that exercise of free will, but there are bound to be consequences when we choose our way over God's. Still, they had been faithful to their promise to fight with the rest of Israel.

In Joshua 22, they were doing something significant to remain part of the whole covenant nation of Israel. They did not want to be cut off from God. And yet they were misunderstood.

7. Have you ever been misunderstood while trying to be faithful?

8. Have you ever jumped to wrong conclusions about someone else?

I'm sure I have been guilty of misjudging others. I am certainly not proud of those moments!

I'm more aware of times when people have jumped to conclusions about my motivations. Every time that happens, my spirit is crushed. Not long ago, I was engaged in helping someone in a ministerial context, only to have someone else (who did not have all of the facts) light into me with cruel accusations. I was unbelievably hurt to learn that anyone would misjudge my character so badly. I had a hard time biting my tongue, and an even harder time facing my accuser the next time I went to church.

Did you catch that? This incident which hurt me so badly happened in the church. I have lost count of how many times people have shared with me that their deepest hurts came from within the church. These occurrences are a serious problem, and I am sure we can take a lesson from Joshua 22. We have all been on both sides of conflicts like the one at Gilgal. We must do better!

9. **No blood was shed at Gilgal, so what was it that brought everyone back to peace?**

10. **What could have made the Gilgal Conflict (I think I just named it that!) better?**

11. **When we are alerted to some wrong another believer has committed (or is believed to have committed), what lesson can we take from Joshua 22 to better honor God in our response?**

I do hope you said we should have a conversation with the other party before leveling accusations. Asking questions and listening to the answers is something we should do a lot more and better!

Read Matthew 18:15-20

12. What steps should Christians take when there is conflict or discord?

Shortly after my recent situation of being misjudged, I was smacked with this lesson: the person who misjudged me is not any sort of authority on who I am. The truth they thought they knew of me was not my truth. My God is my judge. My God knows my character, my intentions, my heart, and my motives. For me to fall apart over something someone says is silly in light of that truth. Still, emotions are what they are, and I did fall apart for a little while, but my heavenly Father scooped me up, hugged me, and set me back on my feet.

13. Can you share a time when you felt the comfort of God after being hurt?

Week 6, Day 3

Joshua's Farewell Speech

We have reached the end of Joshua's time as the leader of Israel. He has served the people as a military leader and as a spiritual leader. He has faithfully communicated to the people what God has communicated to him. And when we pick up today, he is aware that his full and abundant life on earth is about to end. As he was facing his last days, he likely remembered how his mentor Moses spent his final days. Moses took care of the business of affirming Joshua's authority as his successor, reminded the people of the covenant, and wrote out the Law. He did all he could to urge his people to love and obey the Lord.

Read Joshua 23:1-16

1. **What did he want the people to acknowledge? (v.3)**

2. **What did he urge the people to remember? (v.4-5)**

3. What did he want the people to do? (v.6)

4. What was forbidden? (v.7)

5. What was the danger of disobeying? (v.12)

6. What was the great testimony of Joshua's life? (v.14)

Read Joshua 24:1

7. Look at the map, and refer back to our study on Joshua 8:30-35. Why would Joshua choose to renew the covenant at Shechem?

Read Joshua 24:2-13

8. Joshua recites to the people what the Lord has said. **Let's break this up by verses and record what God wanted the people to remember.**

V.2

V.3

V.4

V.5

V.6-**7**

V.8

V.9-**10**

V.11

V.12

V.13

God was summarizing His history with His people beginning with Abraham. Of course, His History with us began when He created us, but this was the beginning of the story of the Nation of Israel, through whom He would bless the whole world. He lists one thing after another which show how He has always been with them, and always been good to them.

9. **If God were to speak to you today in the same way, what would He list as things He has done for you? Include things He did for your ancestors (genetic ancestors/ adopted parents and older generations/ figurative ancestors in the faith) which benefited you as well as miracles you have witnessed for yourself.**

Read Joshua 24:14-15

10. You've just read one of the most quoted statements in Scripture! **Go ahead and write it out yourself if you can claim it as true, or if you choose to declare it as true right now.** *As for me and my house, we will serve the Lord!*

Read Joshua 24:16-28

11. **What did the people claim as their choice?**

Read Joshua 24:29-33

It seems like such a lack-luster description of the end of Joshua's life! But what he did with his life was inspiring. Joshua stands out as one of the very few Bible heroes without a huge moral failure recorded. Abraham lied, Moses' temper revealed a lack of faith, David was an adulterous murderer, and so on, and so on, it goes. Surely, Joshua wasn't perfect, but there is no doubt that the very next thing Joshua experienced was to hear the Lord he has served for so long say something along the lines of, "Well done, good and faithful servant."

Week 6, Day 4

Do Not Be Afraid

A running theme through this study - of Joshua's life - is the repeated phrase, "Do not be afraid." God told Moses to share those words with Joshua, He repeated the words to Joshua more than once, and Joshua and the people reminded each other on many occasions - probably far more often than was recorded for us to read!

Before we close out our study, let's make sure we take this lesson to heart: we need not live in fear, because the Lord our God is with us wherever we go.

1. Look up the following verses and note who gave and received the message, and any details or phrases that stand out to you from these verses.

Isaiah 41:8-14

Jeremiah 1:4-12

Mark 5:35-42

John 14:25-31

Hebrews 13:5-6

2. **Now look up the following verses and write them out as your own prayer.**

Psalm 23:4

Psalm 27:1

Psalm 56:3-4

This truth is a consistent message in Scripture. We serve a God who adores us, and who is mighty and ever-present. He encourages us to live fearlessly, not because of false egos or trust in our greatness, but because we trust Him to be with us and to protect us.

I feel like it cannot be an accident that just today, with this lesson in front of me, I encountered a woman who is struggling with the idea of tithing. Without going into too much detail, the woman was questioning how she could trust God to protect her from further financial hardship after giving Him her money. She asked a tough question that I have heard from so many people: how can she trust God to protect her when she looks around and sees so much unimaginable suffering in the world. So let's look at whether we can trust Him.

Read Genesis 3

Read Romans 5:12

When humanity chose to sin, we brought sin and all of it's ugly, painful consequences into this world, marring God's perfect creation. He didn't do it, we did. Still, there is more to wrestle with.

Read Daniel 3:8-30

3. **God could have chosen to protect these men from being thrown into the fire, but He didn't. What did He do instead?**

Read Genesis 45:5-8

You'll recall from our study in Week One that Joseph's circumstances - from the time his brothers decided to turn on him till many years later - were miserable. He suffered greatly. But even in his suffering, God was with him, and God used his circumstances to bring about something better.

Read Luke 22:39-44

Jesus the Christ, our Savior, God the Son in the flesh prayed to God the Father asking to be delivered from the suffering He knew was imminent.

He was willing to follow the Father's will no matter what, but He asked for another way. However, He is the only way. Though the Father's will allowed for suffering in the flesh that we cringe at, the victory (brought about through Jesus' death and resurrection) was something Jesus was glad to give us.

I don't know why my friend lost her little boy to cancer. I don't know why my cousin died so young. I don't know why another friend's daughter is fighting cancer for the second time in her young life. I don't know why terrorism gets to claim innocent lives. I don't know so, so much. But I do know beyond any shadow of a doubt that God is good, that His plan is ultimately best, He is merciful, even when we can't see or understand, and He can be trusted. Those are among His promises to us.

4. Write out Joshua 23:14, beginning with the second sentence.

Tomorrow we will wrap up our study with a good look at God's promises. Don't miss it!

Seize God's Promises Fearlessly!

We've read through the whole book of Joshua, and then some. We've studied in depth. We've wrestled with difficult scriptures. We've paused to worship our God. We've examined several areas of our lives.

I hope and pray that taking time to work through this study has enriched your understanding of Scripture and God. I pray that it has drawn you closer to Him.

Before we call it quits, I want to give you today to focus on God's promises.

1. **One more time, what was the great testimony of Joshua's life, found in Joshua 23:14?**

This testimony was not only true *for* Joshua; it is true *of* God. God always keeps His promises! Not one of God's good promises has failed!

2. Read the prayer offered by King Solomon at the dedication of the Temple in 1 Kings 8:54-60. What does he say about God's promises?

3. Read Psalm 77. When the psalmist was frustrated and distressed and full of questions, what was his realization (beginning at verse 10)?

4. Look at a few more verses and jot down what you learn about God's promises.

Acts 13:23

Galatians 3:14

1 John 2:25

2 Corinthians 1:20-21

There is no doubt that God is the one we can trust to keep His promises every single time, without fail. Sadly, no human can claim the same. Even with the best of intentions, we can't know the future and circumstances which can make keeping our promises an impossibility.

Read Matthew 5:33-37

5. Why would Jesus say this?

Since the first time I read that, I have tried not to make promises. I have forgotten more times than I can count and made promises I couldn't always keep. I think of the times I made promises to my children, and they never forget those! I haven't always managed to come through. If I asked you to list when people have failed to keep promises they have made to you, you might be drawn to tears so I won't ask! But I think it is safe to declare that we all know humans are not capable of *always* keeping promises without fail. That credit goes to God, alone. While we shouldn't waste our time making promises, we *should* strive for integrity reflecting God's character.

Take some time to think about the promises God has made to you. We looked at some of those promises made in Scripture above. Do you feel like God has made personal promises to you? Before you write anything down, I want to caution you to pray for discernment: we don't want to confuse things we want with actual promises we've received from God.

6. What can you count on as promises from God which apply to you, personally? (Start with those found in Scripture.)

I cannot weigh in on the promises you feel you have received outside of scripture, so for those, if you are in any question (whether it is merely your desire or is really from God), I encourage you to seek godly counsel from someone with a firm grasp of theology. For now, we'll focus on the promises in Scripture.

God's promises to you are there for **you** to seize! Fearlessly! He wants you to live in the light of His promises.

The book of Joshua has been full of exciting battles and victories as Israel claimed the land God had promised. Let them serve as a reminder to seize God's promises fearlessly. Let them also be a reminder to seize God's promises fully! When times are hard, cling to God's promises!

God makes many promises in the pages of Scripture. Read them and know them! Here is just a taste:

> God promises that He loves and adores you. He promises that you are fearfully and wonderfully made. God promises that He has plans for a hope and future for you. He promises to be your steadfast protector. He promises to be true to His character; honest, kind, loving, righteous, and just. He promises to be your healer, your provider, your comforter, your counselor, your source of peace, your source of joy, your salvation, your hope, your refuge, your fortress and strong tower, your banner, your shepherd, your rock, your strength, your Savior, and your guide. He promises that He sees you and that He cares for you. He promises that He is your good Father. He promises that He knows your innermost being, your thoughts, your every action. And He promises that He loves you anyway. He promises that He has provided salvation for you through Jesus Christ. He promises you an eternity with Him if you proclaim that He is the Lord of your Life.

My friend, you are invited by the Almighty One to seize these promises fearlessly!

Week Six Small Group Note Space

Discussion Questions:

Day 1 – 7, 12, 14, 15

Day 2 – 1, 7, 8, 9, 12 (Please don't skip 12!)

Day 3 – 7, 9

Day 4 – Share insights from day 4.

Day 5 – 3, 6

Use this space to record prayer requests and praises from the study group each week.

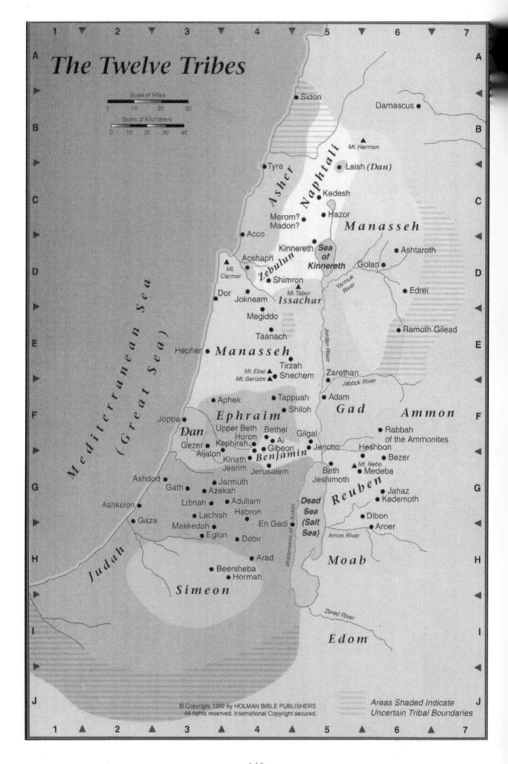

The Twelve Tribes

Scale of Miles
0   10   20   30

Scale of Kilometers
0   10   20   30   40

Sidon

Damascus

Mt. Hermon

Tyre

Asher

Naphtali

Laish (Dan)

Kedesh

Merom?
Madon?

Hazor

Manasseh

Acco

Kinnereth

Sea
of
Kinnereth

Ashtaroth

Acshaph

Golan

Mt.
Carmel

Zebulun

Shimron

Yarmuk
River

Edrei

Dor

Jokneam

Mt. Tabor

Issachar

Megiddo

Ramoth Gilead

Taanach

Jordan River

Hepher

Manasseh

Tirzah

Zarethan

Mt. Ebal
Mt. Gerizim

Shechem

Jabbok River

Mediterranean Sea

(Great Sea)

Aphek

Tappuah

Adam

Gad

Ammon

Joppa

Ephraim

Shiloh

Dan

Upper Beth
Horon

Bethel

Gilgal

Rabbah
of the Ammonites

Gezer

Kephirah

Ai

Jericho

Heshbon

Aijalon

Gibeon

Benjamin

Bezer

Kiriath
Jearim

Mt. Nebo

Ashdod

Jerusalem

Beth
Jeshimoth

Medeba

Jarmuth

Gath

Azekah

Reuben

Jahaz

Ashkelon

Libnah

Adullam

Dead
Sea
(Salt
Sea)

Kedemoth

Gaza

Lachish

Hebron

Dibon

Makkedah

En Gedi

Aroer

Eglon

Debir

Arnon River

Judah

Arad

Moab

Beersheba

Hormah

Simeon

Zered River

Edom

© Copyright 1992 by HOLMAN BIBLE PUBLISHERS
All rights reserved. International Copyright secured.

Areas Shaded Indicate
Uncertain Tribal Boundaries

140

Group Study Leader's Guide

Each member of your study group has the same material. Decide whether the same person will lead the group each week, or if you will take turns.

What does the leader have to do?

- Keep the group informed of any changes in time or location of your gathering.
- Call the group together when it's time to begin.
- The first time you meet, have your group make introductions.
- Be prepared by having done the week's homework.
- Prompt discussion by asking questions or sharing parts of the homework that held your attention.
    - Invite group members to share any insights they had or anything they may feel worth bringing up from their reading.
- Decide how long your group will meet, and do your best to keep to the closing time.

Each week:

- Begin with prayer for focus on what God has to teach you through your group discussion.
- Set the expectation that anything shared in your group is to be treated as confidential.
- Set a time at the end of your group time to share prayer requests and pray together.
- At the end of each week there is a Group Notes page. Certain Questions from the week are indicated there in the hope that they will spark good conversation.
  - You may not have time for all of the questions indicated, so as you prepare by doing the study, mark questions you most want to cover in your group time.

About the Author

Ileana Seward is an author and pastor living in Cincinnati, Ohio. She serves in Women's Ministry, Family Ministry and Biker Ministry. She is on staff at Springdale Church of the Nazarene's Norwood campus and the Cincinnati Salvage Yard Biker Church. She is a wife and a mom. Her passion is to communicate God's redeeming love to broken people.